TIME OUT JOURNAL

MAISON VERO

Published by Maison Vero
3002 Dow Avenue, Suite 112
Tustin, CA 92780

Copyright © 2025 by Matt Doherty
Second Maison Vero hardcover edition November 2025

Maison Vero is a professional publishing house that partners with rising authors to bring their thought leadership to the world. By respecting the copyright of an author's intellectual property, you enable Maison Vero and the author to continue publishing exceptional books for years to come. We thank you for supporting the author's copyright by purchasing an authorized edition of this book.

No amount of this book may be reproduced or stored in any format, nor may it be uploaded to any website, database, language-learning model, or other repository, retrieval, or artificial intelligence system without express permission.
All rights reserved.

Inquiries may be directed to: Maison Vero, 13002 Dow Avenue, Suite 112 Tustin, CA 92780, or info@graymilleragency.com.

For information about special discounts for bulk purchases, please call 1-949-333-4872 or email info@graymilleragency.com.

Maison Vero is a partner brand of The Gray + Miller Agency a speaking, literary, and talent consortium.

For more information on the talent represented by The Gray + Miller Agency, or to bring any of our thought leaders to your organization or live event please visit our website at graymilleragency.com

Manufactured in the United States of America

ISBN 978-1-9695-0800-4

TIME OUT JOURNAL

Reset | Reflect | Grow

MATT DOHERTY

If found, please return it to:

Name:
Address:

Cell:
Email:

*"Whether you think you can, or you think you can't—
you're right."* —Henry Ford

DEDICATION

To God for giving me a blessed life.

To Kelly, Tucker, and Hattie for supporting me on my journey of self-actualization.

WELCOME TO THE TIME OUT JOURNAL

In my journey as an executive coach and host of *The Rebound*, I've had the privilege of speaking with many successful people. One common thread I discovered? They journal. Every day.

Journaling isn't just about writing—it's about reflecting, gaining clarity, and setting the tone for the day ahead. But if you've ever stared at a blank page, unsure of where to start, you're not alone. I've been there, too. My mind would race with to-do lists instead of meaningful reflections. That changed when a coaching client introduced me to a guided journal with prompts that helped me focus. I've used it daily for over a year and a half, and the impact has been profound—more peace, more direction, and a stronger sense of purpose.

Inspired by that experience, I created the *Time Out Journal*—a tool designed to help you pause, reflect, and grow. The way we speak to ourselves shapes our mindset, our actions, and ultimately, our success. Let this journal be a space where you feed yourself thoughts that uplift and empower you.

Wishing you clarity, growth, and fulfillment on your journey.

TABLE OF CONTENTS

INTRODUCTION 1

HOW IT WORKS 5

WHY A "THOUGHT OF THE DAY"? 7

THE POWER OF GRATITUDE 9

THE VALUE OF SETTING GOALS 11

THE POWER OF DAILY AFFIRMATIONS 13

THE VALUE OF THE EVENING TIME OUT 15

THE CHALLENGE 17

THE POWER OF A FRESH START 21

DAILY JOURNAL (DAY 1 - 180) 23

ABOUT THE AUTHOR 215

INTRODUCTION

Welcome to the *Time Out Journal*, a daily tool designed to help you start each morning with clarity, gratitude, and purpose. This journal is inspired by the principles of high-performance leadership, personal growth, and intentional living. By committing just a few minutes each day, you will set the tone for productivity and fulfillment. Daily journaling has been extensively studied in psychology and neuroscience, showing significant benefits for mental clarity, emotional well-being, and personal growth.

Here's the science behind why journaling can be such a powerful tool:

↪ Boosts Mental Clarity and Focus
Writing down thoughts in the morning helps declutter the mind, allowing you to start the day with a clear direction. Neuroscientists suggest that journaling activates the prefrontal cortex, the part of the brain responsible for decision-making and focus. This process enhances cognitive processing, making it easier to prioritize tasks and stay productive throughout the day.

- Enhances Gratitude and Positivity

Studies in positive psychology show that practicing gratitude through journaling can rewire the brain. Expressing gratitude increases dopamine and serotonin levels, the neurotransmitters associated with happiness and emotional well-being. Over time, this strengthens neural pathways that make optimism and resilience more natural.

- Reduces Stress and Anxiety

Writing about emotions helps regulate them. Research by Dr. James Pennebaker at the University of Texas found that expressive writing reduces stress by allowing individuals to process difficult emotions, making them feel less overwhelmed. Journaling also decreases activity in the amygdala, the brain's fear center, reducing anxiety.

- Strengthens Self-Awareness and Emotional Intelligence

Regular self-reflection through journaling enhances emotional intelligence (EQ) by helping individuals understand their emotions, triggers, and thought patterns. This self-awareness leads to better decision-making and stronger interpersonal relationships.

- Builds a Growth Mindset

Journaling about personal development and daily affirmations reinforces a growth mindset, a concept popularized by psychologist Carol Dweck. By focusing on progress and learning, rather than failures, individuals develop greater resilience and a stronger ability to overcome challenges.

- Improves Goal Setting and Achievement

Neuroscientific research shows that writing down goals increases the likelihood of achieving them. Dr. Gail Matthews, a psychology professor at Dominican University, found that people who wrote down their goals were 42% more likely to achieve them compared to those who only thought about them. Writing goals helps the brain filter out distractions and keep priorities in focus.

→ Strengthens Leadership Skills

For leaders, morning journaling fosters self-discipline, strategic thinking, and emotional regulation—all crucial for effective leadership. By setting daily intentions and reflecting on leadership actions, individuals become more intentional in their decision-making and interactions with others.

Final Thought

The science behind journaling is clear: It enhances mental clarity, emotional resilience, and overall well-being. By making it a daily habit, you train your brain to operate at a higher level, setting yourself up for success both personally and professionally. That's why the *Time Out Journal* is designed with these principles in mind—to help you start and end each day with focus, gratitude, and purpose.

HOW IT WORKS

Each day, you'll engage in a simple but powerful routine that includes:

- ↪ Thought of the Day—Seeing one of our favorite and most impactful quotes to inspire your day.
- ↪ Gratitude—Reflect on the good in your life.
- ↪ Goals—Define your "Big 3" goals for a productive day.
- ↪ Daily Affirmations— Reinforce a positive belief about yourself.
- ↪ Evening Time Out—Reflect on your day.

This journal is designed for 180 days. Over time, you will develop habits that elevate your mindset, performance, and leadership. The key is consistency—small daily improvements lead to transformational change.

The *Time Out Journal* is not just a journal—it's a commitment to becoming the best version of yourself. By showing up every day with intention and gratitude, you are taking an active role in shaping your success.

WHY A "THOUGHT OF THE DAY"?

Over the years, I have collected impactful quotes and Bible verses that have inspired me during my journey as a player, coach, and business leader. These words of wisdom have helped me navigate challenges, stay focused on my goals, and keep perspective through both success and adversity.

In creating the *Time Out Journal*, I wanted to share these powerful thoughts with you. Each day, you'll find a "Thought of the Day"—a quote or verse designed to challenge, encourage, or inspire you. Whether it's a reminder to push through adversity, a lesson in leadership, or a moment of spiritual reflection, these words have stood the test of time.

Take a moment each day to reflect on the message. How does it apply to your life? What action can you take? Growth happens in small, intentional steps, and my hope is that these daily thoughts will serve as a guide on your journey.

THE POWER OF GRATITUDE

Gratitude is the practice of recognizing and appreciating the good in our lives. It shifts our focus from what we lack to what we have, creating a mindset of abundance rather than scarcity. When we take time to acknowledge our blessings—big or small—we develop a more positive outlook, strengthen relationships, and improve our overall well-being.

In the *Time Out Journal*, I included a daily space for gratitude because I believe it is one of the most powerful habits for personal growth. No matter what challenges you face, there is always something to be grateful for.

Here are some simple things to appreciate each day:

- Waking up to a new day.
- A kind word from a friend or colleague.
- The warmth of the sun on your face.
- A lesson learned from a challenge.
- The support of loved ones.
- A great cup of coffee.
- The opportunity to grow and improve.

Take a moment each day to write down something you're grateful for. Over time, this simple practice will help you develop a habit of appreciation, leading to a more fulfilling and joyful life.

THE VALUE OF SETTING GOALS

Goals give us direction. They provide a roadmap for our day, helping us stay focused, motivated, and intentional with our time. Without goals, it's easy to drift through the day reacting to circumstances rather than taking control of our actions.

In the *Time Out Journal*, I included a daily space for setting goals (the "Big 3") because I believe that small, consistent steps lead to big results. By starting each day with a clear objective, you set yourself up for success.

Goals don't have to be overwhelming. They can be as simple as:
- Completing an important task at work.
- Making time for exercise.
- Reaching out to a friend or mentor.
- Staying patient in a difficult situation.
- Reading for ten minutes to learn something new.

The key is to be intentional. Take a moment each morning to write down your goals. When you start your day with purpose, you'll find yourself more productive, confident, and fulfilled.

THE POWER OF DAILY AFFIRMATIONS

Your thoughts shape your reality. We all have limiting beliefs that can cripple us. The opposite of limiting beliefs is liberating beliefs. Liberating beliefs empower us to achieve our dreams and goals. What you believe about yourself influences your actions, your confidence, and ultimately, your success. That's why I included a space for liberating beliefs in the *Time Out Journal*—to help you reinforce positive beliefs and develop a strong, resilient mindset.

Affirmations are simple yet powerful statements that remind you of your strengths, values, and potential. When repeated consistently, they help rewire your thinking, replacing doubt and negativity with confidence and purpose.

Here are some examples of liberating beliefs:

- I am strong, capable, and prepared for any challenge.
- I bring value to those around me.
- I am constantly learning and growing.
- I choose to focus on solutions, not obstacles.
- I have the discipline to achieve my goals.

Start each day by writing a liberating belief that speaks to you. Over time, this habit will help you develop a more positive, focused, and resilient mindset - one that will push you toward your goals and help you navigate life's challenges with confidence.

THE VALUE OF THE EVENING TIME OUT

Reflection is one of the most powerful tools for growth. Taking a few moments at the end of each day to evaluate your experiences helps you recognize progress, learn from challenges, and prepare for a better tomorrow. That's why I included an Evening Time Out section in the *Time Out Journal*—to encourage you to pause, reflect, and grow.

A good evening time out should include:

- Highlights—What were the best moments of your day? A win at work, a great conversation, or simply a moment of joy?
- Lessons Learned—What challenged you today?
  What would you do differently next time?
- Progress Toward Goals—Did you take steps toward your personal or professional goals (the "Big 3")?
  What adjustments need to be made?

Here are some simple reflection prompts:

- What am I most proud of today?
- What is one thing I learned?
- How did I step outside my comfort zone?
- What could I improve on for tomorrow?

By making reflection a daily habit, you'll become more intentional, self-aware, and prepared for future success. Growth doesn't happen by accident—it happens through learning from experience and applying those lessons moving forward.

THE CHALLENGE

Starting a new habit takes commitment, and journaling is no different. But the benefits of reflection, goal-setting, and gratitude are worth it. By taking on this challenge, you are making a promise to yourself—to grow, to learn, and to become more intentional with your time and energy.

To help you get started, I highly recommend that you write down your commitment. See the example below. There is a blank challenge form for you to fill out on the next page.

I, Matt Doherty, commit to writing in the *Time Out Journal* every day for the next seven days.

Journaling is important to me because: I want to feed myself with positive thoughts to help me become the best version of myself.

When I finish writing in the *Time Out Journal* for seven consecutive days, I will celebrate by: Taking my wife out for a nice dinner.

If I don't complete seven days in a row, I will donate $100 to my favorite charity, which is: The Charlotte Rescue Mission.

<u>I will create a habit of journaling every day by doing the following:</u>

- I will put the journal and a pen next to my sink.
- I will write in the journal in the morning, right when I get out of bed.
- I will wake up ten minutes early to write in my journal.
- I will write in my journal every night before I go to bed.

By taking this challenge, you are setting yourself up for success. The key is consistency. Keep your journal in a visible place, set a reminder, and make it part of your routine—just like brushing your teeth or having your morning coffee.

Stick with it, and you'll be amazed at the clarity, focus, and motivation you gain.

Want more tips and resources? Visit www.dohertycoaching.com to learn more.

The Challenge Form

I, _____, commit to journaling in the *Time Out Journal* every day for the next seven days.

Journaling is important to me because:

When I finish writing in the *Time Out Journal* for seven consecutive days, I will celebrate by:

If I don't complete seven days in a row, I will donate $100 to my favorite charity, which is:

I will create a habit of journaling every day by doing the following:

❶ _____

❷ _____

❸ _____

❹ _____

Here is an example of how to complete your daily journal:

DAY 1   DATE: 01 / 01 / 2025

"Whether you think you can, or you think you can't — you're right." —Henry Ford

I am grateful for the following things in my life: **A.M.**

My beautiful kids

My wonderful life

The opportunity to work with wonderful people

I will accomplish my "Big 3" today:

I will work out for thirty minutes.

I will make three prospecting calls.

I will not eat sweets.

This liberating belief will empower me today:

I can accomplish anything I set my mind to.

Highlights of my day: **P.M.**

Great 1-2-1 sessions with my clients.

Lessons learned:

How to incorporate artificial intelligence for proposals.

Did I accomplish my "Big 3" today? If not, why?

No. I was 2 for 3 today because I cheated and had

several chocolate chip cookies.

THE POWER OF A FRESH START

I remember walking into the Dean Smith Center on my first day as the head coach of the University of North Carolina. The echoes of greatness were in those walls—Michael Jordan, James Worthy, Coach Smith himself. It was intimidating, but it was also a fresh start. I wasn't the assistant at Kansas. I wasn't the head coach at Notre Dame. I wasn't the player from the '82 championship team. I was starting a new chapter, and the expectations were sky-high.

But here's what I realized—a fresh start doesn't mean perfection. It means embracing the opportunity to begin again, with new lessons, new challenges, and a renewed commitment. Every day, we have that same chance. You don't need a title change, a new job, or a major life event to start fresh. You just need the decision to let go of yesterday's baggage.

We all have days we wish we could redo—mistakes we made, words we regret, opportunities we missed. But holding onto those moments doesn't help us grow. Progress isn't about flawless execution; it's about consistent effort.

Reflection:

↪ What do you need to let go of from yesterday?
↪ How will you show up differently today?
↪ What's one small action you can take to reset and refocus?

Today is your fresh start. Make it count.

DAILY JOURNAL (DAY 1 - 180)

DAY 1 DATE: ___ / ___ / ____

"The most important thing about your life isn't the year you were born or the year you died. It's what you did in the dash."
—Steve Wilson's dad

I am grateful for the following things in my life: **A.M.**

_____
_____
_____

I will accomplish my "Big 3" today:

_____
_____
_____

This liberating belief will empower me today:

_____
_____
_____

Highlights of my day: **P.M.**

_____
_____
_____

Lessons learned:

_____
_____
_____

Did I accomplish my "Big 3" today? If not, why?

_____
_____

DAY 2   DATE: ___ / ___ / ___

"Service to others is the rent you pay for your room here on earth." —Muhammad Ali

I am grateful for the following things in my life: **A.M.**

_____
_____
_____

I will accomplish my "Big 3" today:

_____
_____
_____

This liberating belief will empower me today:

_____
_____

Highlights of my day: **P.M.**

_____
_____
_____

Lessons learned:

_____
_____
_____

Did I accomplish my "Big 3" today? If not, why?

_____
_____

DAY 3   DATE: ___ / ___ / ___

"I'm a great believer in luck, and I find the harder I work the more I have of it." — Thomas Jefferson

I am grateful for the following things in my life: **A.M.**

_____
_____
_____

I will accomplish my "Big 3" today:

_____
_____
_____

This liberating belief will empower me today:

_____
_____
_____

Highlights of my day: **P.M.**

_____
_____
_____

Lessons learned:

_____
_____
_____

Did I accomplish my "Big 3" today? If not, why?

_____
_____

DAY 4   DATE: ___ / ___ / ____

"Here's how I'm going to beat you. I'm going to outwork you. That's it. That's all there is to it." —Pat Summitt

I am grateful for the following things in my life: **A.M.**

_____

_____

_____

I will accomplish my "Big 3" today:

_____

_____

_____

This liberating belief will empower me today:

_____

_____

Highlights of my day: **P.M.**

_____

_____

_____

Lessons learned:

_____

_____

_____

Did I accomplish my "Big 3" today? If not, why?

_____

_____

DAY 5   DATE: ___ / ___ / ____

"Don't count the days; make the days count."
—*Muhammad Ali*

I am grateful for the following things in my life: **A.M.**

_____
_____
_____

I will accomplish my "Big 3" today:

_____
_____
_____

This liberating belief will empower me today:

_____
_____
_____

Highlights of my day: **P.M.**

_____
_____
_____

Lessons learned:

_____
_____
_____

Did I accomplish my "Big 3" today? If not, why?

_____
_____

DAY 6   DATE: ___ / ___ / ___

"My best skill was that I was coachable. I was a sponge and aggressive to learn." —Michael Jordan

I am grateful for the following things in my life: **A.M.**

_____
_____
_____

I will accomplish my "Big 3" today:

_____
_____
_____

This liberating belief will empower me today:

_____
_____
_____

Highlights of my day: **P.M.**

_____
_____
_____

Lessons learned:

_____
_____
_____

Did I accomplish my "Big 3" today? If not, why?

_____
_____

DAY 7   DATE: ___ / ___ / ____

"Admit to and make yourself accountable for mistakes. How can you improve if you're never wrong?" —Pat Summitt

🛡 I am grateful for the following things in my life: **A.M.**

_____
_____
_____

I will accomplish my "Big 3" today:

_____
_____
_____

This liberating belief will empower me today:

_____
_____
_____

🛡 Highlights of my day: **P.M.**

_____
_____
_____

Lessons learned:

_____
_____
_____

Did I accomplish my "Big 3" today? If not, why?

_____
_____

Congratulations! You Did It!

 A message from Coach Doherty

You set a goal, showed up for yourself, and completed seven consecutive days of journaling. That's a big deal! Taking time each day to reflect, refocus, and realign is a powerful step toward becoming the leader—and person—you want to be. Now, it's time to celebrate!

How will you honor this accomplishment?

Look back at "The Challenge" page and remind yourself of how you were going to celebrate this milestone, and do it! Acknowledging your progress helps reinforce the habit and builds momentum for the next challenge ahead.

Reflection:

- ➢ What have I learned about myself in the past week?
- ➢ How has journaling impacted my mindset, focus, or clarity?
- ➢ What's one small shift I've noticed in my leadership, work, or personal life?

This is just the beginning. Keep going—you're building something great. On to the next streak!

DAY 8   DATE: ___ / ___ / ____

"There are seven days in the week and 'someday' isn't one of them." —Benny Lewis

I am grateful for the following things in my life: **A.M.**

_____
_____
_____

I will accomplish my "Big 3" today:

_____
_____
_____

This liberating belief will empower me today:

_____
_____

Highlights of my day: **P.M.**

_____
_____
_____

Lessons learned:

_____
_____
_____

Did I accomplish my "Big 3" today? If not, why?

_____
_____

DAY 9   DATE: ___ / ___ / ____

"A truly wise person uses few words; a person with understanding is even-tempered." —Proverbs 17:27

I am grateful for the following things in my life: **A.M.**

_____
_____
_____

I will accomplish my "Big 3" today:

_____
_____
_____

This liberating belief will empower me today:

_____
_____

Highlights of my day: **P.M.**

_____
_____
_____

Lessons learned:

_____
_____
_____

Did I accomplish my "Big 3" today? If not, why?

_____
_____

DAY 10 DATE: ___ / ___ / ____

"As we advance in our careers, behavioral changes are often the only significant changes we can make." —Marshall Goldsmith

A.M. I am grateful for the following things in my life:

___

___

I will accomplish my "Big 3" today:

___

___

This liberating belief will empower me today:

___

___

P.M. Highlights of my day:

___

___

Lessons learned:

___

___

Did I accomplish my "Big 3" today? If not, why?

___

___

DAY 11   DATE: ___ / ___ / ____

"Enthusiasm is common. Endurance is rare."
—Angela Duckworth

I am grateful for the following things in my life: **A.M.**

_____

_____

_____

I will accomplish my "Big 3" today:

_____

_____

_____

This liberating belief will empower me today:

_____

_____

Highlights of my day: **P.M.**

_____

_____

_____

Lessons learned:

_____

_____

_____

Did I accomplish my "Big 3" today? If not, why?

_____

_____

DAY 12   DATE: ___ / ___ / _____

"You can sweep it under the rug until it gets so big you trip over it." —Rick Omohundro

I am grateful for the following things in my life: **A.M.**

_____
_____
_____

I will accomplish my "Big 3" today:

_____
_____
_____

This liberating belief will empower me today:

_____
_____
_____

Highlights of my day: **P.M.**

_____
_____
_____

Lessons learned:

_____
_____
_____

Did I accomplish my "Big 3" today? If not, why?

_____
_____

DAY 13   DATE: ___ / ___ / ____

"The difference between average people and achieving people is their perception of and response to failure." —John C. Maxwell

I am grateful for the following things in my life: **A.M.**

_____
_____
_____

I will accomplish my "Big 3" today:

_____
_____
_____

This liberating belief will empower me today:

_____
_____

Highlights of my day: **P.M.**

_____
_____
_____

Lessons learned:

_____
_____
_____

Did I accomplish my "Big 3" today? If not, why?

_____
_____

DAY 14   DATE: ___ / ___ / _____

"Being nervous isn't bad. It just means something important is happening." —Michael Jordan

I am grateful for the following things in my life: **A.M.**

_____
_____
_____

I will accomplish my "Big 3" today:

_____
_____
_____

This liberating belief will empower me today:

_____
_____
_____

Highlights of my day: **P.M.**

_____
_____
_____

Lessons learned:

_____
_____
_____

Did I accomplish my "Big 3" today? If not, why?

_____
_____

14 Days: The Habit is Taking Hold

 A message from Coach Doherty

You've made it two weeks—and that matters more than you might realize.

Research shows that habit formation begins with consistency. The early days are where most people stumble... but not you! You've shown up, page after page, and that effort is already reshaping how you think, lead, and live.

This isn't just about journaling it's—about becoming the kind of person who follows through.

You're no longer hoping to get better... you're training to get better.

Let this be a reminder:

- ➢ Small actions repeated daily lead to big results.
- ➢ Reflection builds clarity.
- ➢ Routine becomes identity.

Keep writing. Keep reflecting. Keep growing.

Your 14-day streak is proof: you're building something powerful—one page at a time.

DAY 15   DATE: ___ / ___ / ____

"Pain is inevitable. Suffering is optional."
—*Haruki Murakami*

I am grateful for the following things in my life: **A.M.**

_____
_____
_____

I will accomplish my "Big 3" today:

_____
_____
_____

This liberating belief will empower me today:

_____
_____

Highlights of my day: **P.M.**

_____
_____
_____

Lessons learned:

_____
_____
_____

Did I accomplish my "Big 3" today? If not, why?

_____
_____

DAY 16   DATE: ___ / ___ / ____

"Time and energy are limited. Any successful person has to decide on what to do in part by deciding what not to do."
—Angela Duckworth

I am grateful for the following things in my life: **A.M.**

_____
_____
_____

I will accomplish my "Big 3" today:

_____
_____
_____

This liberating belief will empower me today:

_____
_____

Highlights of my day: **P.M.**

_____
_____
_____

Lessons learned:

_____
_____
_____

Did I accomplish my "Big 3" today? If not, why?

_____
_____

DAY 17   DATE: ___ / ___ / ____

"Always forgive your enemies; nothing annoys them so much."
—Oscar Wilde

I am grateful for the following things in my life: **A.M.**

_____
_____
_____

I will accomplish my "Big 3" today:

_____
_____
_____

This liberating belief will empower me today:

_____
_____
_____

Highlights of my day: **P.M.**

_____
_____
_____

Lessons learned:

_____
_____
_____

Did I accomplish my "Big 3" today? If not, why?

_____
_____

DAY 18   DATE: ___ / ___ / ___

"Fools show their annoyance at once, but the prudent overlook an insult." —Proverbs 12:16

I am grateful for the following things in my life: **A.M.**

_____
_____
_____

I will accomplish my "Big 3" today:

_____
_____
_____

This liberating belief will empower me today:

_____
_____
_____

Highlights of my day: **P.M.**

_____
_____
_____

Lessons learned:

_____
_____
_____

Did I accomplish my "Big 3" today? If not, why?

_____
_____

DAY 19 DATE: ___ / ___ / _____

"Done is better than perfect."
— *Unknown*

I am grateful for the following things in my life: **A.M.**

_____
_____
_____

I will accomplish my "Big 3" today:

_____
_____
_____

This liberating belief will empower me today:

_____
_____

Highlights of my day: **P.M.**

_____
_____
_____

Lessons learned:

_____
_____
_____

Did I accomplish my "Big 3" today? If not, why?

_____
_____

DAY 20   DATE: ___ / ___ / _____

"Knowing yourself is the beginning of all wisdom."
—Aristotle

I am grateful for the following things in my life: **A.M.**

_____
_____
_____

I will accomplish my "Big 3" today:

_____
_____
_____

This liberating belief will empower me today:

_____
_____

Highlights of my day: **P.M.**

_____
_____
_____

Lessons learned:

_____
_____
_____

Did I accomplish my "Big 3" today? If not, why?

_____
_____

DAY 21   DATE: ___ / ___ / ____

"The two most important days in your life: The day you were born, and the day you find out why." —John Maxwell

I am grateful for the following things in my life: **A.M.**

_____
_____
_____

I will accomplish my "Big 3" today:

_____
_____
_____

This liberating belief will empower me today:

_____
_____
_____

Highlights of my day: **P.M.**

_____
_____
_____

Lessons learned:

_____
_____
_____

Did I accomplish my "Big 3" today? If not, why?

_____
_____

21 Days: You've Built It

 A message from Coach Doherty

You didn't just start something—you stuck with it. That matters. For three straight weeks, you've shown up, pen in hand, page after page. Not out of obligation...but out of intention.

By now, you're not just trying to journal—you're becoming someone who does.

This is the identity shift that separates dabblers from doers. The hardest part of any new discipline is making it stick. You've done that. Now you have momentum—and momentum is gold.

DAY 22   DATE: ___ / ___ / ___

"The day you think you have it mastered is the day you start your decline." —Tim Hofferth

I am grateful for the following things in my life: **A.M.**

_____
_____
_____

I will accomplish my "Big 3" today:

_____
_____
_____

This liberating belief will empower me today:

_____
_____

Highlights of my day: **P.M.**

_____
_____
_____

Lessons learned:

_____
_____
_____

Did I accomplish my "Big 3" today? If not, why?

_____
_____

DAY 23   DATE: ___ / ___ / _____

"The best do ordinary things better than everyone else."
— Chuck Noll

I am grateful for the following things in my life: **A.M.**

_____

_____

_____

I will accomplish my "Big 3" today:

_____

_____

_____

This liberating belief will empower me today:

_____

_____

_____

Highlights of my day: **P.M.**

_____

_____

_____

Lessons learned:

_____

_____

_____

Did I accomplish my "Big 3" today? If not, why?

_____

_____

DAY 24   DATE: ___ / ___ / ____

"Your time is limited, so don't waste it living someone else's life." —Steve Jobs

I am grateful for the following things in my life: **A.M.**

_____
_____
_____

I will accomplish my "Big 3" today:

_____
_____
_____

This liberating belief will empower me today:

_____
_____

Highlights of my day: **P.M.**

_____
_____
_____

Lessons learned:

_____
_____
_____

Did I accomplish my "Big 3" today? If not, why?

_____
_____

DAY 25   DATE: ___ / ___ / _____

"The greatest enemies of peace are anxiety and worry."
—Cammie Howard

I am grateful for the following things in my life: **A.M.**

_____
_____
_____

I will accomplish my "Big 3" today:

_____
_____
_____

This liberating belief will empower me today:

_____
_____

Highlights of my day: **P.M.**

_____
_____
_____

Lessons learned:

_____
_____
_____

Did I accomplish my "Big 3" today? If not, why?

_____
_____

DAY 26   DATE: ___ / ___ / ____

"Nothing is really work unless you would rather be doing something else." —J.M. Barrie

I am grateful for the following things in my life: **A.M.**

_____
_____
_____

I will accomplish my "Big 3" today:

_____
_____
_____

This liberating belief will empower me today:

_____
_____
_____

Highlights of my day: **P.M.**

_____
_____
_____

Lessons learned:

_____
_____
_____

Did I accomplish my "Big 3" today? If not, why?

_____
_____

DAY 27   DATE: ___ / ___ / ____

"Be patient with yourself. Self-growth is tender; it's holy ground. There's no greater investment." —Stephen Covey

I am grateful for the following things in my life: **A.M.**

_____
_____
_____

I will accomplish my "Big 3" today:

_____
_____
_____

This liberating belief will empower me today:

_____
_____

Highlights of my day: **P.M.**

_____
_____
_____

Lessons learned:

_____
_____
_____

Did I accomplish my "Big 3" today? If not, why?

_____
_____

DAY 28 DATE: ___ / ___ / _____

"He who knows, does not speak. He who speaks, does not know." —Lao Tzu

I am grateful for the following things in my life: **A.M.**

_____
_____
_____

I will accomplish my "Big 3" today:

_____
_____
_____

This liberating belief will empower me today:

_____
_____
_____

Highlights of my day: **P.M.**

_____
_____
_____

Lessons learned:

_____
_____
_____

Did I accomplish my "Big 3" today? If not, why?

_____
_____

DAY 29   DATE: ___ / ___ / _____

"Whoever disregards discipline comes to poverty and shame, but whoever heeds correction is honored." —Proverbs 13:18

I am grateful for the following things in my life: **A.M.**

_____
_____
_____

I will accomplish my "Big 3" today:

_____
_____
_____

This liberating belief will empower me today:

_____
_____
_____

Highlights of my day: **P.M.**

_____
_____
_____

Lessons learned:

_____
_____
_____

Did I accomplish my "Big 3" today? If not, why?

_____
_____

DAY 30   DATE: ___ / ___ / ____

"Don't blow out your own candle."
—*Paul Martinelli*

I am grateful for the following things in my life: **A.M.**

_____
_____
_____

I will accomplish my "Big 3" today:

_____
_____
_____

This liberating belief will empower me today:

_____
_____
_____

Highlights of my day: **P.M.**

_____
_____
_____

Lessons learned:

_____
_____
_____

Did I accomplish my "Big 3" today? If not, why?

_____
_____

Growth Comes from Discomfort

 A message from Coach Doherty

I'll never forget the press conference when I resigned from UNC. It was one of the most painful moments of my life. I felt exposed, embarrassed, and like I had failed. But looking back, that discomfort was the catalyst for my growth.

In the months that followed, I had to sit with hard truths about my leadership style, my blind spots, and my resilience. It would've been easy to play the victim, but instead, I leaned into the discomfort. I read, reflected, and sought feedback. It was in the struggle that I found clarity.

Growth isn't comfortable. It challenges your ego, tests your patience, and pushes you to places you'd rather avoid. But discomfort is where transformation lives.

Reflection:

➢ What challenge are you facing right now that feels uncomfortable?

➢ What lesson might it be trying to teach you?

➢ How can you lean into the discomfort instead of avoiding it?

Remember, comfort zones don't build leaders—discomfort does.

DAY 31   DATE: ___ / ___ / ____

"Many are the plans in a person's heart, but it is the Lord's purpose that prevails." —Proverbs 19:21

🛡   I am grateful for the following things in my life: **A.M.**

_____
_____
_____

I will accomplish my "Big 3" today:

_____
_____
_____

This liberating belief will empower me today:

_____
_____

🛡   Highlights of my day: **P.M.**

_____
_____
_____

Lessons learned:

_____
_____
_____

Did I accomplish my "Big 3" today? If not, why?

_____
_____

DAY 32   DATE: ___ / ___ / ____

"True courage is being afraid and going ahead and doing your job anyhow." —Norman Schwarzkopf

I am grateful for the following things in my life: **A.M.**

_____
_____
_____

I will accomplish my "Big 3" today:

_____
_____
_____

This liberating belief will empower me today:

_____
_____

Highlights of my day: **P.M.**

_____
_____
_____

Lessons learned:

_____
_____
_____

Did I accomplish my "Big 3" today? If not, why?

_____
_____

DAY 33   DATE: ___ / ___ / ____

"If you can't measure it, you can't improve it."
— Peter Drucker

I am grateful for the following things in my life: **A.M.**

_____
_____
_____

I will accomplish my "Big 3" today:

_____
_____
_____

This liberating belief will empower me today:

_____
_____
_____

Highlights of my day: **P.M.**

_____
_____
_____

Lessons learned:

_____
_____
_____

Did I accomplish my "Big 3" today? If not, why?

_____
_____

DAY 34   DATE: ___ / ___ / ___

"The meaning of life is to find your gift. The purpose of life is to give it away." — Pablo Picasso

I am grateful for the following things in my life: **A.M.**

_____

_____

_____

I will accomplish my "Big 3" today:

_____

_____

_____

This liberating belief will empower me today:

_____

_____

Highlights of my day: **P.M.**

_____

_____

_____

Lessons learned:

_____

_____

_____

Did I accomplish my "Big 3" today? If not, why?

_____

_____

DAY 35   DATE: ___ / ___ / ____

"Do not answer a fool according to his folly, or you yourself will be just like him." —Proverbs 26:4

I am grateful for the following things in my life: **A.M.**

_____
_____
_____

I will accomplish my "Big 3" today:

_____
_____
_____

This liberating belief will empower me today:

_____
_____
_____

Highlights of my day: **P.M.**

_____
_____
_____

Lessons learned:

_____
_____
_____

Did I accomplish my "Big 3" today? If not, why?

_____
_____

DAY 36 DATE: ___ / ___ / _____

"There is no greater agony than bearing an untold story inside you." —Maya Angelou

I am grateful for the following things in my life: **A.M.**

_____
_____
_____

I will accomplish my "Big 3" today:

_____
_____
_____

This liberating belief will empower me today:

_____
_____
_____

Highlights of my day: **P.M.**

_____
_____
_____

Lessons learned:

_____
_____
_____

Did I accomplish my "Big 3" today? If not, why?

_____
_____

DAY 37   DATE: ___ / ___ / ____

"The only job security you have is your individual commitment to personal development." —Kevin Turner

I am grateful for the following things in my life: **A.M.**

_____
_____
_____

I will accomplish my "Big 3" today:

_____
_____
_____

This liberating belief will empower me today:

_____
_____

Highlights of my day: **P.M.**

_____
_____
_____

Lessons learned:

_____
_____
_____

Did I accomplish my "Big 3" today? If not, why?

_____
_____

DAY 38   DATE: ___ / ___ / ____

"The race will go to the curious, the slightly mad."
—*Tom Peters*

I am grateful for the following things in my life: **A.M.**

_____
_____
_____

I will accomplish my "Big 3" today:

_____
_____
_____

This liberating belief will empower me today:

_____
_____

Highlights of my day: **P.M.**

_____
_____
_____

Lessons learned:

_____
_____
_____

Did I accomplish my "Big 3" today? If not, why?

_____
_____

DAY 39   DATE: ___ / ___ / ____

"You grow at the end of your comfort zone."
—John Maxwell

I am grateful for the following things in my life: **A.M.**

_____
_____
_____

I will accomplish my "Big 3" today:

_____
_____
_____

This liberating belief will empower me today:

_____
_____
_____

Highlights of my day: **P.M.**

_____
_____
_____

Lessons learned:

_____
_____
_____

Did I accomplish my "Big 3" today? If not, why?

_____
_____

DAY 40   DATE: ___ / ___ / _____

"People are anxious to improve their circumstances, but they are unwilling to improve themselves." —James Allen

I am grateful for the following things in my life: **A.M.**

_____
_____
_____

I will accomplish my "Big 3" today:

_____
_____
_____

This liberating belief will empower me today:

_____
_____

Highlights of my day: **P.M.**

_____
_____
_____

Lessons learned:

_____
_____
_____

Did I accomplish my "Big 3" today? If not, why?

_____
_____

DAY 41   DATE: ___ / ___ / _____

"Every pain introduces a person to themselves."
—John Locke

🛡 I am grateful for the following things in my life: **A.M.**

_____
_____
_____

I will accomplish my "Big 3" today:

_____
_____
_____

This liberating belief will empower me today:

_____
_____

🛡   Highlights of my day: **P.M.**

_____
_____
_____

Lessons learned:

_____
_____
_____

Did I accomplish my "Big 3" today? If not, why?

_____
_____

DAY 42   DATE: ___ / ___ / ___

"Nothing is more confusing than people who give good advice, but set a bad example." —Norman Vincent Peale

I am grateful for the following things in my life: **A.M.**

_____
_____
_____

I will accomplish my "Big 3" today:

_____
_____
_____

This liberating belief will empower me today:

_____
_____
_____

Highlights of my day: **P.M.**

_____
_____
_____

Lessons learned:

_____
_____
_____

Did I accomplish my "Big 3" today? If not, why?

_____
_____

DAY 43   DATE: ___ / ___ / ____

"I have a Ph.D. in failing, but a master's in getting back up."
—Alex Rodriguez

I am grateful for the following things in my life: **A.M.**

_____
_____
_____

I will accomplish my "Big 3" today:

_____
_____
_____

This liberating belief will empower me today:

_____
_____
_____

Highlights of my day: **P.M.**

_____
_____
_____

Lessons learned:

_____
_____
_____

Did I accomplish my "Big 3" today? If not, why?

_____
_____

DAY 44   DATE: ___ / ___ / ____

"Don't compare your everyday to another's highlight reel!"
— *Steven Furtick*

I am grateful for the following things in my life: **A.M.**

_____
_____
_____

I will accomplish my "Big 3" today:

_____
_____
_____

This liberating belief will empower me today:

_____
_____

Highlights of my day: **P.M.**

_____
_____
_____

Lessons learned:

_____
_____
_____

Did I accomplish my "Big 3" today? If not, why?

_____
_____

DAY 45   DATE: ___ / ___ / ___

"When there is a void in communication, the default emotion is negative." —Matt Doherty

🛡   I am grateful for the following things in my life: **A.M.**

_____
_____
_____

I will accomplish my "Big 3" today:

_____
_____
_____

This liberating belief will empower me today:

_____
_____

🛡   Highlights of my day: **P.M.**

_____
_____
_____

Lessons learned:

_____
_____
_____

Did I accomplish my "Big 3" today? If not, why?

_____
_____

DAY 46　　　　DATE: ___ / ___ / ___

"Have you ever regretted a selfless act?"
— *Unknown*

I am grateful for the following things in my life:　　**A.M.**

_____
_____
_____

I will accomplish my "Big 3" today:

_____
_____
_____

This liberating belief will empower me today:

_____
_____

Highlights of my day:　　**P.M.**

_____
_____
_____

Lessons learned:

_____
_____
_____

Did I accomplish my "Big 3" today? If not, why?

_____
_____

DAY 47   DATE: ___ / ___ / _____

"I never lose. I either win or I learn."
—Nelson Mandela

I am grateful for the following things in my life: **A.M.**

_____
_____
_____

I will accomplish my "Big 3" today:

_____
_____
_____

This liberating belief will empower me today:

_____
_____
_____

Highlights of my day: **P.M.**

_____
_____
_____

Lessons learned:

_____
_____
_____

Did I accomplish my "Big 3" today? If not, why?

_____
_____

DAY 48   DATE: ___ / ___ / ____

"Enjoy the little things in life, for one day you may look back and realize they were the big things." —Robert Brault

I am grateful for the following things in my life: **A.M.**

_____
_____
_____

I will accomplish my "Big 3" today:

_____
_____
_____

This liberating belief will empower me today:

_____
_____

Highlights of my day: **P.M.**

_____
_____
_____

Lessons learned:

_____
_____
_____

Did I accomplish my "Big 3" today? If not, why?

_____
_____

DAY 49 DATE: ___ / ___ / ____

"We can't always choose the music life plays for us, but we can choose how we dance to it!" —Anonymous

I am grateful for the following things in my life: **A.M.**

_____
_____
_____

I will accomplish my "Big 3" today:

_____
_____
_____

This liberating belief will empower me today:

_____
_____
_____

Highlights of my day: **P.M.**

_____
_____
_____

Lessons learned:

_____
_____
_____

Did I accomplish my "Big 3" today? If not, why?

_____
_____

DAY 50   DATE: ___ / ___ / _____

"One of the most sincere forms of respect is actually listening to what another has to say." —Bryant H. McGill

I am grateful for the following things in my life: **A.M.**

_____
_____
_____

I will accomplish my "Big 3" today:

_____
_____
_____

This liberating belief will empower me today:

_____
_____

Highlights of my day: **P.M.**

_____
_____
_____

Lessons learned:

_____
_____
_____

Did I accomplish my "Big 3" today? If not, why?

_____
_____

DAY 51 DATE: ___ / ___ / ___

"Laughter is an instant vacation."
—Milton Berle

I am grateful for the following things in my life: **A.M.**

_____
_____
_____

I will accomplish my "Big 3" today:

_____
_____
_____

This liberating belief will empower me today:

_____
_____
_____

Highlights of my day: **P.M.**

_____
_____
_____

Lessons learned:

_____
_____
_____

Did I accomplish my "Big 3" today? If not, why?

_____
_____

DAY 52   DATE: ___ / ___ / ____

"The key is not to prioritize what's on your schedule, but to schedule your priorities." —Stephen Covey

I am grateful for the following things in my life: **A.M.**

_____

_____

_____

I will accomplish my "Big 3" today:

_____

_____

_____

This liberating belief will empower me today:

_____

_____

Highlights of my day: **P.M.**

_____

_____

_____

Lessons learned:

_____

_____

_____

Did I accomplish my "Big 3" today? If not, why?

_____

_____

DAY 53　　　　　DATE: ___ / ___ / ____

"Say 'Yes' to the fire that burns inside you."
— Sorin Popa

I am grateful for the following things in my life:　　**A.M.**

_____
_____
_____

I will accomplish my "Big 3" today:

_____
_____
_____

This liberating belief will empower me today:

_____
_____
_____

Highlights of my day:　　**P.M.**

_____
_____
_____

Lessons learned:

_____
_____
_____

Did I accomplish my "Big 3" today? If not, why?

_____
_____

DAY 54   DATE: ___ / ___ / ___

"Don't make an agreement with your limitations."
—Paul Martinelli

I am grateful for the following things in my life: **A.M.**

_____
_____
_____

I will accomplish my "Big 3" today:

_____
_____
_____

This liberating belief will empower me today:

_____
_____

Highlights of my day: **P.M.**

_____
_____
_____

Lessons learned:

_____
_____
_____

Did I accomplish my "Big 3" today? If not, why?

_____
_____

DAY 55 DATE: ___ / ___ / _____

"Your life is impacted by three things... the people you meet, the books you read, and the trauma in your life."
—*Matt Doherty*

I am grateful for the following things in my life: **A.M.**

_____
_____
_____

I will accomplish my "Big 3" today:

_____
_____
_____

This liberating belief will empower me today:

_____
_____
_____

Highlights of my day: **P.M.**

_____
_____
_____

Lessons learned:

_____
_____
_____

Did I accomplish my "Big 3" today? If not, why?

_____
_____

DAY 56   DATE: ___ / ___ / ____

"Don't wait until someone's funeral to say nice things to them." — Unknown

I am grateful for the following things in my life: **A.M.**

_____

_____

_____

I will accomplish my "Big 3" today:

_____

_____

_____

This liberating belief will empower me today:

_____

_____

Highlights of my day: **P.M.**

_____

_____

_____

Lessons learned:

_____

_____

_____

Did I accomplish my "Big 3" today? If not, why?

_____

_____

DAY 57 DATE: ___ / ___ / _____

"A lion doesn't concern himself with the opinions of the sheep."
— *Tywin Lannister*

I am grateful for the following things in my life: **A.M.**

_____
_____
_____

I will accomplish my "Big 3" today:

_____
_____
_____

This liberating belief will empower me today:

_____
_____

Highlights of my day: **P.M.**

_____
_____
_____

Lessons learned:

_____
_____
_____

Did I accomplish my "Big 3" today? If not, why?

_____
_____

DAY 58　　　DATE: ___ / ___ / ____

*"When something bad happens you have three choices:
You can let it define you, you can let it destroy you, or you can let it strengthen you. Choose wisely!"* —Unknown

I am grateful for the following things in my life:　**A.M.**

_____
_____
_____

I will accomplish my "Big 3" today:

_____
_____
_____

This liberating belief will empower me today:

_____
_____
_____

Highlights of my day:　**P.M.**

_____
_____
_____

Lessons learned:

_____
_____
_____

Did I accomplish my "Big 3" today? If not, why?

_____
_____

DAY 59   DATE: ___ / ___ / ___

"Success is walking from failure to failure with no loss of enthusiasm." —Winston Churchill

I am grateful for the following things in my life: **A.M.**

_____
_____
_____

I will accomplish my "Big 3" today:

_____
_____
_____

This liberating belief will empower me today:

_____
_____
_____

Highlights of my day: **P.M.**

_____
_____
_____

Lessons learned:

_____
_____
_____

Did I accomplish my "Big 3" today? If not, why?

_____
_____

DAY 60   DATE: ___ / ___ / ___

"Never argue with a fool. Onlookers may not be able to tell the difference." —Mark Twain

I am grateful for the following things in my life: **A.M.**

_____

_____

_____

I will accomplish my "Big 3" today:

_____

_____

_____

This liberating belief will empower me today:

_____

_____

Highlights of my day: **P.M.**

_____

_____

_____

Lessons learned:

_____

_____

_____

Did I accomplish my "Big 3" today? If not, why?

_____

_____

Small Habits, Big Results

A message from Coach Doherty

When I played at UNC, Coach Dean Smith had a rule: Always point to the teammate who passed you the ball after a made shot. It was a small gesture, easy to overlook. But that tiny habit created a culture of gratitude, connection, and team-first thinking.

In leadership and life, it's the small habits that compound into big results. Whether it's showing up on time, reading 10 pages a day, or taking five minutes to reflect—those daily choices shape who you become.

After my coaching career, I committed to reading every day. It didn't seem like much at first, but over time, it transformed my mindset, my leadership approach, and ultimately, my career as an executive coach. Consistency beats intensity when it comes to habits.

Reflection:

- What small habit could you start today that aligns with your goals?
- How can you create a simple routine to make it stick?
- Remember: it's not about doing it perfectly, it's about showing up daily.

Remember, comfort zones don't build leaders—discomfort does.

DAY 61   DATE: ___ / ___ / _____

"Choices lead to habits. Habits become talents. Talents are labeled gifts. You're not born this way, you get this way."
—Seth Godin

I am grateful for the following things in my life: **A.M.**

_____
_____
_____

I will accomplish my "Big 3" today:

_____
_____
_____

This liberating belief will empower me today:

_____
_____

Highlights of my day: **P.M.**

_____
_____
_____

Lessons learned:

_____
_____
_____

Did I accomplish my "Big 3" today? If not, why?

_____
_____

DAY 62 DATE: ___ / ___ / ___

"You choose your thoughts."
— Paul Martinelli

I am grateful for the following things in my life: **A.M.**

_____
_____
_____

I will accomplish my "Big 3" today:

_____
_____
_____

This liberating belief will empower me today:

_____
_____

Highlights of my day: **P.M.**

_____
_____
_____

Lessons learned:

_____
_____
_____

Did I accomplish my "Big 3" today? If not, why?

_____
_____

DAY 63   DATE: ___ / ___ / ____

"Listen with the intent to understand."
—John Maxwell

I am grateful for the following things in my life: **A.M.**

I will accomplish my "Big 3" today:

This liberating belief will empower me today:

Highlights of my day: **P.M.**

Lessons learned:

Did I accomplish my "Big 3" today? If not, why?

DAY 64   DATE: ___ / ___ / ____

"Trust in the Lord with all thine heart; and lean not unto thine own understanding. In all thy ways acknowledge him, and He shall direct thy paths." —Proverbs 3:5-6

I am grateful for the following things in my life: **A.M.**

_____
_____
_____

I will accomplish my "Big 3" today:

_____
_____
_____

This liberating belief will empower me today:

_____
_____

Highlights of my day: **P.M.**

_____
_____
_____

Lessons learned:

_____
_____
_____

Did I accomplish my "Big 3" today? If not, why?

_____
_____

DAY 65 DATE: ___ / ___ / _____

"In matters of style, swim with the current. In matters of principle, stand like a rock." — *Thomas Jefferson*

I am grateful for the following things in my life: **A.M.**

_____
_____
_____

I will accomplish my "Big 3" today:

_____
_____
_____

This liberating belief will empower me today:

_____
_____

Highlights of my day: **P.M.**

_____
_____
_____

Lessons learned:

_____
_____
_____

Did I accomplish my "Big 3" today? If not, why?

_____
_____

DAY 66   DATE: ___ / ___ / ____

"Leave the woodpile higher than you found it."
—Ric Elias

I am grateful for the following things in my life: **A.M.**

_____
_____
_____

I will accomplish my "Big 3" today:

_____
_____
_____

This liberating belief will empower me today:

_____
_____
_____

Highlights of my day: **P.M.**

_____
_____
_____

Lessons learned:

_____
_____
_____

Did I accomplish my "Big 3" today? If not, why?

_____
_____

DAY 67 DATE: ___ / ___ / ____

"Happiness begins where selfishness ends."
—John Wooden

I am grateful for the following things in my life: **A.M.**

_____
_____
_____

I will accomplish my "Big 3" today:

_____
_____
_____

This liberating belief will empower me today:

_____
_____

Highlights of my day: **P.M.**

_____
_____
_____

Lessons learned:

_____
_____
_____

Did I accomplish my "Big 3" today? If not, why?

_____
_____

DAY 68 DATE: ___ / ___ / ___

"Effective communication values the recipient over the sender."
—*Neil Gordon*

I am grateful for the following things in my life: **A.M.**

_____
_____
_____

I will accomplish my "Big 3" today:

_____
_____
_____

This liberating belief will empower me today:

_____
_____
_____

Highlights of my day: **P.M.**

_____
_____
_____

Lessons learned:

_____
_____
_____

Did I accomplish my "Big 3" today? If not, why?

_____
_____

DAY 69　　　DATE: ___ / ___ / ____

"Everything you want is on the other side of hard."
—Monty Williams

🛡 I am grateful for the following things in my life:　　**A.M.**

_____
_____
_____

I will accomplish my "Big 3" today:

_____
_____
_____

This liberating belief will empower me today:

_____
_____

🛡　　　　Highlights of my day:　　　　**P.M.**

_____
_____
_____

Lessons learned:

_____
_____
_____

Did I accomplish my "Big 3" today? If not, why?

_____
_____

DAY 70   DATE: ___ / ___ / ____

"You can act your way into a new way of thinking quicker than you can think your way into a new way of acting."
—Dr. Richard Pascale

I am grateful for the following things in my life: **A.M.**

_____
_____
_____

I will accomplish my "Big 3" today:

_____
_____
_____

This liberating belief will empower me today:

_____
_____

Highlights of my day: **P.M.**

_____
_____
_____

Lessons learned:

_____
_____
_____

Did I accomplish my "Big 3" today? If not, why?

_____
_____

DAY 71   DATE: ___ / ___ / ____

"Nervousness and excitement are opposite sides of the same coin." —Nan Doherty

I am grateful for the following things in my life: **A.M.**

_____
_____
_____

I will accomplish my "Big 3" today:

_____
_____
_____

This liberating belief will empower me today:

_____
_____

Highlights of my day: **P.M.**

_____
_____
_____

Lessons learned:

_____
_____
_____

Did I accomplish my "Big 3" today? If not, why?

_____
_____

DAY 72 DATE: ___ / ___ / _____

"There is a difference between listening and waiting for your turn to speak." —Simon Sinek

I am grateful for the following things in my life: **A.M.**

_____
_____
_____

I will accomplish my "Big 3" today:

_____
_____
_____

This liberating belief will empower me today:

_____
_____

Highlights of my day: **P.M.**

_____
_____
_____

Lessons learned:

_____
_____
_____

Did I accomplish my "Big 3" today? If not, why?

_____
_____

DAY 73 DATE: ___ / ___ / ____

"Weak people seek revenge. Strong people forgive. Intelligent people ignore." —Albert Einstein

I am grateful for the following things in my life: **A.M.**

_____
_____
_____

I will accomplish my "Big 3" today:

_____
_____
_____

This liberating belief will empower me today:

_____
_____

Highlights of my day: **P.M.**

_____
_____
_____

Lessons learned:

_____
_____
_____

Did I accomplish my "Big 3" today? If not, why?

_____
_____

DAY 74   DATE: ___ / ___ / ____

"What we think we become!"
—Buddha

I am grateful for the following things in my life: **A.M.**

_____
_____
_____

I will accomplish my "Big 3" today:

_____
_____
_____

This liberating belief will empower me today:

_____
_____
_____

Highlights of my day: **P.M.**

_____
_____
_____

Lessons learned:

_____
_____
_____

Did I accomplish my "Big 3" today? If not, why?

_____
_____

DAY 75 DATE: ___ / ___ / ___

"Mine for the truth."
—Matt Doherty

I am grateful for the following things in my life: **A.M.**

_____
_____
_____

I will accomplish my "Big 3" today:

_____
_____
_____

This liberating belief will empower me today:

_____
_____

Highlights of my day: **P.M.**

_____
_____
_____

Lessons learned:

_____
_____
_____

Did I accomplish my "Big 3" today? If not, why?

_____
_____

DAY 76   DATE: ___ / ___ / _____

"If you rearrange the letters from the word 'depression' you get 'I pressed on!' Your current situation doesn't have to be your final destination." —Joyce Meyer

I am grateful for the following things in my life: **A.M.**

___

I will accomplish my "Big 3" today:

___

This liberating belief will empower me today:

___

Highlights of my day: **P.M.**

___

Lessons learned:

___

Did I accomplish my "Big 3" today? If not, why?

DAY 77   DATE: ___ / ___ / _____

"I've got my faults, but living in the past isn't one of them. There's no future in it!" —Sparky Anderson

I am grateful for the following things in my life: **A.M.**

_____

_____

_____

I will accomplish my "Big 3" today:

_____

_____

_____

This liberating belief will empower me today:

_____

_____

Highlights of my day: **P.M.**

_____

_____

_____

Lessons learned:

_____

_____

_____

Did I accomplish my "Big 3" today? If not, why?

_____

_____

DAY 78   DATE: ___ / ___ / ____

"If you want to go fast, go alone. If you want to go far, go together." —African Proverb

I am grateful for the following things in my life: **A.M.**

_____
_____

I will accomplish my "Big 3" today:

_____
_____

This liberating belief will empower me today:

_____
_____

Highlights of my day: **P.M.**

_____
_____

Lessons learned:

_____
_____

Did I accomplish my "Big 3" today? If not, why?

_____
_____

DAY 79   DATE: ___ / ___ / ____

"You don't rise to the occasion. You fall to the level of your training." —Navy Seals

I am grateful for the following things in my life: **A.M.**

I will accomplish my "Big 3" today:

This liberating belief will empower me today:

Highlights of my day: **P.M.**

Lessons learned:

Did I accomplish my "Big 3" today? If not, why?

DAY 80   DATE: ___ / ___ / ____

"You might be on the right track, but if you are standing still you will get run over." —Will Rogers

🛡 I am grateful for the following things in my life: **A.M.**

_____
_____
_____

I will accomplish my "Big 3" today:

_____
_____
_____

This liberating belief will empower me today:

_____
_____
_____

🛡   Highlights of my day: **P.M.**

_____
_____
_____

Lessons learned:

_____
_____
_____

Did I accomplish my "Big 3" today? If not, why?

_____
_____

DAY 81 DATE: ___ / ___ / _____

"It is never too late to be what you might have been."
—George Eliot

I am grateful for the following things in my life: **A.M.**

_____
_____
_____

I will accomplish my "Big 3" today:

_____
_____
_____

This liberating belief will empower me today:

_____
_____
_____

Highlights of my day: **P.M.**

_____
_____
_____

Lessons learned:

_____
_____
_____

Did I accomplish my "Big 3" today? If not, why?

_____
_____

DAY 82 DATE: ___ / ___ / ___

"You never outperform your self-beliefs."
—Paul Martinelli

I am grateful for the following things in my life: **A.M.**

_____
_____
_____

I will accomplish my "Big 3" today:

_____
_____
_____

This liberating belief will empower me today:

_____
_____
_____

Highlights of my day: **P.M.**

_____
_____
_____

Lessons learned:

_____
_____
_____

Did I accomplish my "Big 3" today? If not, why?

_____
_____

DAY 83   DATE: ___ / ___ / _____

"The truth is that we all experience pain in our lives, but I believe that the problems we face are our opportunity and define our human purpose." — Steve Gleason

I am grateful for the following things in my life: **A.M.**

_____
_____
_____

I will accomplish my "Big 3" today:

_____
_____
_____

This liberating belief will empower me today:

_____
_____

Highlights of my day: **P.M.**

_____
_____
_____

Lessons learned:

_____
_____
_____

Did I accomplish my "Big 3" today? If not, why?

_____
_____

DAY 84 DATE: ___ / ___ / ____

"Disagree without being disagreeable."
—Zig Ziglar

I am grateful for the following things in my life: **A.M.**

_____
_____

I will accomplish my "Big 3" today:

_____
_____

This liberating belief will empower me today:

_____
_____

Highlights of my day: **P.M.**

_____
_____

Lessons learned:

_____
_____

Did I accomplish my "Big 3" today? If not, why?

_____
_____

DAY 85   DATE: ___ / ___ / ____

"It won't be easy, but it will be worth it!"
—Kyle Shanahan

A.M.

I am grateful for the following things in my life:

_____
_____
_____

I will accomplish my "Big 3" today:

_____
_____
_____

This liberating belief will empower me today:

_____
_____

P.M.

Highlights of my day:

_____
_____
_____

Lessons learned:

_____
_____
_____

Did I accomplish my "Big 3" today? If not, why?

_____
_____

DAY 86 DATE: ___ / ___ / ____

"Honesty is the first chapter in the book of wisdom."
—*Thomas Jefferson*

I am grateful for the following things in my life: **A.M.**

_____
_____
_____

I will accomplish my "Big 3" today:

_____
_____
_____

This liberating belief will empower me today:

_____
_____
_____

Highlights of my day: **P.M.**

_____
_____
_____

Lessons learned:

_____
_____
_____

Did I accomplish my "Big 3" today? If not, why?

_____
_____

DAY 87   DATE: ___ / ___ / _____

"Hard work isn't punishment. Hard work is the price of admission for the opportunity to reach excellence." —Jay Bilas

I am grateful for the following things in my life: **A.M.**

_____
_____
_____

I will accomplish my "Big 3" today:

_____
_____
_____

This liberating belief will empower me today:

_____
_____
_____

Highlights of my day: **P.M.**

_____
_____
_____

Lessons learned:

_____
_____
_____

Did I accomplish my "Big 3" today? If not, why?

_____
_____

DAY 88   DATE: ___ / ___ / ___

"It's one of the greatest gifts you can give yourself, to forgive. Forgive everybody." —Maya Angelou

A.M. I am grateful for the following things in my life:

_____
_____
_____

I will accomplish my "Big 3" today:

_____
_____
_____

This liberating belief will empower me today:

_____
_____
_____

P.M. Highlights of my day:

_____
_____
_____

Lessons learned:

_____
_____
_____

Did I accomplish my "Big 3" today? If not, why?

_____
_____

DAY 89 DATE: ___ / ___ / ____

*"I have self-doubt. I have insecurity. I have fear of failure...
You don't capitulate to it. You embrace it."* —Kobe Bryant

I am grateful for the following things in my life: **A.M.**

_____
_____
_____

I will accomplish my "Big 3" today:

_____
_____
_____

This liberating belief will empower me today:

_____
_____
_____

Highlights of my day: **P.M.**

_____
_____
_____

Lessons learned:

_____
_____
_____

Did I accomplish my "Big 3" today? If not, why?

_____
_____

DAY 90 DATE: ___ / ___ / _____

"Live as if you were to die tomorrow. Learn as if you were to live forever." —Gandhi

I am grateful for the following things in my life: **A.M.**

_____
_____
_____

I will accomplish my "Big 3" today:

_____
_____
_____

This liberating belief will empower me today:

_____
_____
_____

Highlights of my day: **P.M.**

_____
_____
_____

Lessons learned:

_____
_____
_____

Did I accomplish my "Big 3" today? If not, why?

_____
_____

Reflection

A message from
Coach Doherty

Take a moment to assess your progress. Are you closer to your goals than you were three months ago? What habits have served you well, and what needs adjusting? Growth doesn't happen by chance—it happens by choice. If you need a coach in your corner to push, challenge, and support you, visit www.dohertycoaching.com to take the next step.

DAY 91   DATE: ___ / ___ / ____

"Speak when you are angry and you will make the best speech you will ever regret." —Ambrose Bierce

🛡   I am grateful for the following things in my life: **A.M.**

_____
_____
_____

I will accomplish my "Big 3" today:

_____
_____
_____

This liberating belief will empower me today:

_____
_____
_____

🛡   Highlights of my day: **P.M.**

_____
_____
_____

Lessons learned:

_____
_____
_____

Did I accomplish my "Big 3" today? If not, why?

_____
_____

DAY 92   DATE: ___ / ___ / ____

*"Wise men speak because they have something to say;
Fools because they have to say something."* —Plato

I am grateful for the following things in my life: **A.M.**

_____
_____
_____

I will accomplish my "Big 3" today:

_____
_____
_____

This liberating belief will empower me today:

_____
_____

Highlights of my day: **P.M.**

_____
_____
_____

Lessons learned:

_____
_____
_____

Did I accomplish my "Big 3" today? If not, why?

_____
_____

DAY 93   DATE: ___ / ___ / ___

"Hard is the way."
—Bruce Lee

I am grateful for the following things in my life: **A.M.**

_____
_____
_____

I will accomplish my "Big 3" today:

_____
_____
_____

This liberating belief will empower me today:

_____
_____
_____

Highlights of my day: **P.M.**

_____
_____
_____

Lessons learned:

_____
_____
_____

Did I accomplish my "Big 3" today? If not, why?

_____
_____

DAY 94 DATE: ___ / ___ / _____

"A gossip betrays a confidence, but a trustworthy person keeps a secret." —Proverbs 11:13

I am grateful for the following things in my life: **A.M.**

___

I will accomplish my "Big 3" today:

___

This liberating belief will empower me today:

___

Highlights of my day: **P.M.**

___

Lessons learned:

___

Did I accomplish my "Big 3" today? If not, why?

DAY 95   DATE: ___ / ___ / ___

"If you get the dirty end of the stick, sharpen it and turn it into a useful tool." —Colin Powell

I am grateful for the following things in my life: **A.M.**

_____
_____
_____

I will accomplish my "Big 3" today:

_____
_____
_____

This liberating belief will empower me today:

_____
_____

Highlights of my day: **P.M.**

_____
_____

Lessons learned:

_____
_____
_____

Did I accomplish my "Big 3" today? If not, why?

_____
_____

DAY 96   DATE: ___ / ___ / ___

> *"Comparison is the thief of joy."*
> — *Theodore Roosevelt*

I am grateful for the following things in my life: **A.M.**

_____
_____
_____

I will accomplish my "Big 3" today:

_____
_____
_____

This liberating belief will empower me today:

_____
_____

Highlights of my day: **P.M.**

_____
_____
_____

Lessons learned:

_____
_____
_____

Did I accomplish my "Big 3" today? If not, why?

_____
_____

DAY 97 DATE: ___ / ___ / _____

"Our greatest weakness lies in giving up. The most certain way to succeed is always to try just one more time."
—Thomas Edison

I am grateful for the following things in my life: **A.M.**

_____
_____
_____

I will accomplish my "Big 3" today:

_____
_____
_____

This liberating belief will empower me today:

_____
_____

Highlights of my day: **P.M.**

_____
_____
_____

Lessons learned:

_____
_____
_____

Did I accomplish my "Big 3" today? If not, why?

_____
_____

DAY 98   DATE: ___ / ___ / _____

"The world gives us worry, but Jesus gives us peace."
—Cammie Howard

I am grateful for the following things in my life: **A.M.**

_____
_____
_____

I will accomplish my "Big 3" today:

_____
_____
_____

This liberating belief will empower me today:

_____
_____
_____

Highlights of my day: **P.M.**

_____
_____
_____

Lessons learned:

_____
_____
_____

Did I accomplish my "Big 3" today? If not, why?

_____
_____

DAY 99   DATE: ___ / ___ / _____

"Either run the day or the day runs you."
—Jim Rohn

I am grateful for the following things in my life: **A.M.**

_____
_____
_____

I will accomplish my "Big 3" today:

_____
_____
_____

This liberating belief will empower me today:

_____
_____

Highlights of my day: **P.M.**

_____
_____
_____

Lessons learned:

_____
_____
_____

Did I accomplish my "Big 3" today? If not, why?

_____
_____

DAY 100   DATE: ___ / ___ / ___

*"Manage the truth or the truth will manage you...
right out the door."* —Matt Doherty

I am grateful for the following things in my life: **A.M.**

_____
_____
_____

I will accomplish my "Big 3" today:

_____
_____
_____

This liberating belief will empower me today:

_____
_____

Highlights of my day: **P.M.**

_____
_____
_____

Lessons learned:

_____
_____
_____

Did I accomplish my "Big 3" today? If not, why?

_____
_____

DAY 101   DATE: ___ / ___ / _____

"Cowards die many times before their deaths; the valiant never taste of death but once." —William Shakespeare

I am grateful for the following things in my life: **A.M.**

_____
_____
_____

I will accomplish my "Big 3" today:

_____
_____
_____

This liberating belief will empower me today:

_____
_____
_____

Highlights of my day: **P.M.**

_____
_____
_____

Lessons learned:

_____
_____
_____

Did I accomplish my "Big 3" today? If not, why?

_____
_____

DAY 102 DATE: ___ / ___ / ___

"Are the habits you have today on par with the dreams you have for tomorrow?" —Alan Stein, Jr

I am grateful for the following things in my life: **A.M.**

_____
_____
_____

I will accomplish my "Big 3" today:

_____
_____
_____

This liberating belief will empower me today:

_____
_____

Highlights of my day: **P.M.**

_____
_____
_____

Lessons learned:

_____
_____
_____

Did I accomplish my "Big 3" today? If not, why?

_____
_____

DAY 103   DATE: ___ / ___ / ____

"Don't tell me about your dreams of a castle, show me the stones you laid today." —Wayne Bryan

I am grateful for the following things in my life: **A.M.**

_____
_____
_____

I will accomplish my "Big 3" today:

_____
_____
_____

This liberating belief will empower me today:

_____
_____
_____

Highlights of my day: **P.M.**

_____
_____
_____

Lessons learned:

_____
_____
_____

Did I accomplish my "Big 3" today? If not, why?

_____
_____

DAY 104   DATE: ___ / ___ / _____

"Almost everything will work again if you unplug it for a few minutes, including you." —Anne Lamott

I am grateful for the following things in my life: **A.M.**

_____
_____
_____

I will accomplish my "Big 3" today:

_____
_____
_____

This liberating belief will empower me today:

_____
_____

Highlights of my day: **P.M.**

_____
_____

Lessons learned:

_____
_____
_____

Did I accomplish my "Big 3" today? If not, why?

_____
_____

DAY 105   DATE: ___ / ___ / ____

"Fools show their annoyance at once, but the prudent overlook an insult." —Proverbs 12:16

I am grateful for the following things in my life: **A.M.**

_____
_____
_____

I will accomplish my "Big 3" today:

_____
_____
_____

This liberating belief will empower me today:

_____
_____

Highlights of my day: **P.M.**

_____
_____
_____

Lessons learned:

_____
_____
_____

Did I accomplish my "Big 3" today? If not, why?

_____
_____

DAY 106　　DATE: ___ / ___ / _____

"Like a slingshot, the way forward often means you have to go backward first. There will be tension and stress."
—Pastor Jerel Law

I am grateful for the following things in my life:　**A.M.**

_____
_____
_____

I will accomplish my "Big 3" today:

_____
_____
_____

This liberating belief will empower me today:

_____
_____
_____

Highlights of my day:　**P.M.**

_____
_____
_____

Lessons learned:

_____
_____
_____

Did I accomplish my "Big 3" today? If not, why?

_____
_____

DAY 107   DATE: ___ / ___ / ____

"I hated every minute of training, but I said, 'Don't quit. Suffer now and live the rest of your life as a champion.'"
—Muhammad Ali

I am grateful for the following things in my life: **A.M.**

_____
_____
_____

I will accomplish my "Big 3" today:

_____
_____
_____

This liberating belief will empower me today:

_____
_____

Highlights of my day: **P.M.**

_____
_____
_____

Lessons learned:

_____
_____
_____

Did I accomplish my "Big 3" today? If not, why?

_____
_____

DAY 108   DATE: ___ / ___ / _____

"A single conversation across the table with a wise man is better than ten years of mere study of books."
—Henry Wadsworth Longfellow

I am grateful for the following things in my life: **A.M.**

_____
_____
_____

I will accomplish my "Big 3" today:

_____
_____
_____

This liberating belief will empower me today:

_____
_____

Highlights of my day: **P.M.**

_____
_____
_____

Lessons learned:

_____
_____
_____

Did I accomplish my "Big 3" today? If not, why?

_____
_____

DAY 109　　　DATE: ___ / ___ / ___

"I would rather adjust my life to your absence than adjust my boundaries to accommodate your disrespect." —John Lucas

I am grateful for the following things in my life:　**A.M.**

_____
_____

I will accomplish my "Big 3" today:

_____
_____

This liberating belief will empower me today:

_____
_____

Highlights of my day:　**P.M.**

_____
_____

Lessons learned:

_____
_____

Did I accomplish my "Big 3" today? If not, why?

_____
_____

DAY 110 DATE: ___ / ___ / ____

"One man makes a majority."
—Andrew Jackson

I am grateful for the following things in my life: **A.M.**

_____
_____
_____

I will accomplish my "Big 3" today:

_____
_____
_____

This liberating belief will empower me today:

_____
_____

Highlights of my day: **P.M.**

_____
_____
_____

Lessons learned:

_____
_____
_____

Did I accomplish my "Big 3" today? If not, why?

_____
_____

DAY 111   DATE: ___ / ___ / ____

"Fear is a reaction. Courage is a decision."
—Winston Churchill

I am grateful for the following things in my life: **A.M.**

_____
_____
_____

I will accomplish my "Big 3" today:

_____
_____
_____

This liberating belief will empower me today:

_____
_____

Highlights of my day: **P.M.**

_____
_____
_____

Lessons learned:

_____
_____
_____

Did I accomplish my "Big 3" today? If not, why?

_____
_____

DAY 112   DATE: ___ / ___ / _____

"Humble yourselves, therefore, under God's mighty hand, that He may lift you up in due time. Cast all your anxiety on Him because He cares for you." —1 Peter 5:6-7

🛡 I am grateful for the following things in my life: **A.M.**

_____
_____
_____

I will accomplish my "Big 3" today:

_____
_____
_____

This liberating belief will empower me today:

_____
_____

🛡 Highlights of my day: **P.M.**

_____
_____
_____

Lessons learned:

_____
_____
_____

Did I accomplish my "Big 3" today? If not, why?

_____
_____

DAY 113   DATE: ___ / ___ / ____

"Today is the only day. Yesterday is gone."
—John Wooden

I am grateful for the following things in my life: **A.M.**

_____
_____
_____

I will accomplish my "Big 3" today:

_____
_____
_____

This liberating belief will empower me today:

_____
_____

Highlights of my day: **P.M.**

_____
_____
_____

Lessons learned:

_____
_____
_____

Did I accomplish my "Big 3" today? If not, why?

_____
_____

DAY 114   DATE: ___ / ___ / ___

"I like the dreams of the future better than the history of the past." — Thomas Jefferson

I am grateful for the following things in my life: **A.M.**

_____
_____
_____

I will accomplish my "Big 3" today:

_____
_____
_____

This liberating belief will empower me today:

_____
_____

Highlights of my day: **P.M.**

_____
_____
_____

Lessons learned:

_____
_____
_____

Did I accomplish my "Big 3" today? If not, why?

_____
_____

DAY 115 DATE: ___ / ___ / ____

"No man is rich enough to buy back his past."
—Oscar Wilde

I am grateful for the following things in my life: **A.M.**

_____
_____
_____

I will accomplish my "Big 3" today:

_____
_____
_____

This liberating belief will empower me today:

_____
_____
_____

Highlights of my day: **P.M.**

_____
_____
_____

Lessons learned:

_____
_____
_____

Did I accomplish my "Big 3" today? If not, why?

_____
_____

DAY 116 DATE: ___ / ___ / ___

> *"Life is a sum of all your choices."*
> —Albert Camus

I am grateful for the following things in my life: **A.M.**

_____
_____
_____

I will accomplish my "Big 3" today:

_____
_____
_____

This liberating belief will empower me today:

_____
_____

Highlights of my day: **P.M.**

_____
_____
_____

Lessons learned:

_____
_____
_____

Did I accomplish my "Big 3" today? If not, why?

_____
_____

DAY 117 DATE: ___ / ___ / ____

"When we are no longer able to change a situation, we are challenged to change ourselves." —Viktor Frankl

I am grateful for the following things in my life: **A.M.**

I will accomplish my "Big 3" today:

This liberating belief will empower me today:

Highlights of my day: **P.M.**

Lessons learned:

Did I accomplish my "Big 3" today? If not, why?

DAY 118   DATE: ___ / ___ / ____

"God, grant me the serenity to accept the things I cannot change, the courage to change the things I can, and the wisdom to know the difference." —Serenity Prayer

I am grateful for the following things in my life: **A.M.**

_____
_____
_____

I will accomplish my "Big 3" today:

_____
_____
_____

This liberating belief will empower me today:

_____
_____

Highlights of my day: **P.M.**

_____
_____
_____

Lessons learned:

_____
_____
_____

Did I accomplish my "Big 3" today? If not, why?

_____
_____

DAY 119   DATE: ___ / ___ / ____

"You bring the weather."
—Matt Doherty

I am grateful for the following things in my life: **A.M.**

_____
_____
_____

I will accomplish my "Big 3" today:

_____
_____
_____

This liberating belief will empower me today:

_____
_____
_____

Highlights of my day: **P.M.**

_____
_____
_____

Lessons learned:

_____
_____
_____

Did I accomplish my "Big 3" today? If not, why?

_____
_____

DAY 120   DATE: ___ / ___ / ___

"Never regret. If it's good, it's wonderful. If it's bad, it's experience." —Victoria Holt

I am grateful for the following things in my life: **A.M.**

___

I will accomplish my "Big 3" today:

___

This liberating belief will empower me today:

___

Highlights of my day: **P.M.**

___

Lessons learned:

___

Did I accomplish my "Big 3" today? If not, why?

___

Reflection

A message from Coach Doherty

Sometimes, we don't lack talent or effort—we lack the right strategy. Are you facing obstacles that seem impossible to overcome? Often, an outside perspective can help unlock new solutions. If you're ready to break through barriers and elevate your leadership, let's talk. Contact www.dohertycoaching.com to help you grow.

DAY 121   DATE: ___ / ___ / ____

"When a man doesn't know what harbor he is making for, no wind is the right wind." —Seneca

I am grateful for the following things in my life: **A.M.**

_____
_____
_____

I will accomplish my "Big 3" today:

_____
_____
_____

This liberating belief will empower me today:

_____
_____

Highlights of my day: **P.M.**

_____
_____
_____

Lessons learned:

_____
_____
_____

Did I accomplish my "Big 3" today? If not, why?

_____
_____

DAY 122 DATE: ___ / ___ / ___

"Stress is the trash of modern life—we all generate it but if you don't dispose of it properly, it will pile up and overtake your life." —Terri Guillemets

I am grateful for the following things in my life: **A.M.**

___

I will accomplish my "Big 3" today:

___

This liberating belief will empower me today:

___

Highlights of my day: **P.M.**

___

Lessons learned:

___

Did I accomplish my "Big 3" today? If not, why?

DAY 123   DATE: ___ / ___ / ____

*"Mass movements don't start with the masses.
They start with the few." —John Maxwell*

I am grateful for the following things in my life: **A.M.**

_____
_____
_____

I will accomplish my "Big 3" today:

_____
_____
_____

This liberating belief will empower me today:

_____
_____

Highlights of my day: **P.M.**

_____
_____
_____

Lessons learned:

_____
_____
_____

Did I accomplish my "Big 3" today? If not, why?

_____
_____

DAY 124 DATE: ___ / ___ / _____

"We're in control of our attitude. Good or bad. Your choice. Everything in life prepares us for the moment we're in right now." —Ted Nolan

I am grateful for the following things in my life: **A.M.**

_____
_____
_____

I will accomplish my "Big 3" today:

_____
_____
_____

This liberating belief will empower me today:

_____
_____
_____

Highlights of my day: **P.M.**

_____
_____
_____

Lessons learned:

_____
_____
_____

Did I accomplish my "Big 3" today? If not, why?

_____
_____

DAY 125   DATE: ___ / ___ / _____

"The more you invest the harder it is to surrender."
—*Anonymous*

I am grateful for the following things in my life: **A.M.**

_____
_____
_____

I will accomplish my "Big 3" today:

_____
_____
_____

This liberating belief will empower me today:

_____
_____

Highlights of my day: **P.M.**

_____
_____
_____

Lessons learned:

_____
_____
_____

Did I accomplish my "Big 3" today? If not, why?

_____
_____

DAY 126   DATE: ___ / ___ / ____

"Dreams are never fulfilled in your comfort zone."
—George Raveling

I am grateful for the following things in my life: **A.M.**

_____
_____

I will accomplish my "Big 3" today:

_____
_____

This liberating belief will empower me today:

_____
_____

Highlights of my day: **P.M.**

_____
_____

Lessons learned:

_____
_____

Did I accomplish my "Big 3" today? If not, why?

_____
_____

DAY 127　　　　DATE: ___ / ___ / ____

"Sloppiness is a disease."
—Bob McKillop

I am grateful for the following things in my life:　**A.M.**

_____
_____
_____

I will accomplish my "Big 3" today:

_____
_____
_____

This liberating belief will empower me today:

_____
_____
_____

Highlights of my day:　**P.M.**

_____
_____
_____

Lessons learned:

_____
_____
_____

Did I accomplish my "Big 3" today? If not, why?

_____
_____

DAY 128　　　　DATE: ___ / ___ / ____

"It's better to have a thousand enemies outside the tent than one inside the tent." —Ancient Proverb

I am grateful for the following things in my life:　　**A.M.**

_____
_____
_____

I will accomplish my "Big 3" today:

_____
_____
_____

This liberating belief will empower me today:

_____
_____
_____

Highlights of my day:　　**P.M.**

_____
_____
_____

Lessons learned:

_____
_____
_____

Did I accomplish my "Big 3" today? If not, why?

_____
_____

DAY 129   DATE: ___ / ___ / ___

"JP Morgan's guaranteed formula for success; ❶ *Every morning, write a list of things that need to be done that day.* ❷ *Do them."*

I am grateful for the following things in my life: **A.M.**

___

I will accomplish my "Big 3" today:

___

This liberating belief will empower me today:

___

Highlights of my day: **P.M.**

___

Lessons learned:

___

Did I accomplish my "Big 3" today? If not, why?

___

DAY 130   DATE: ___ / ___ / _____

"The 1st stage of learning is silence, the second stage is listening." —Aristotle

I am grateful for the following things in my life: **A.M.**

_____
_____
_____

I will accomplish my "Big 3" today:

_____
_____
_____

This liberating belief will empower me today:

_____
_____
_____

Highlights of my day: **P.M.**

_____
_____
_____

Lessons learned:

_____
_____
_____

Did I accomplish my "Big 3" today? If not, why?

_____
_____

DAY 131　　　　DATE: ___ / ___ / ____

"Do common things uncommonly well."
—John D. Rockefeller

🛡 I am grateful for the following things in my life:　**A.M.**

_____
_____
_____

I will accomplish my "Big 3" today:

_____
_____
_____

This liberating belief will empower me today:

_____
_____

🛡 Highlights of my day:　**P.M.**

_____
_____
_____

Lessons learned:

_____
_____
_____

Did I accomplish my "Big 3" today? If not, why?

_____
_____

DAY 132   DATE: ___ / ___ / ____

"Great minds discuss ideas; average minds discuss events; small minds discuss people." —Eleanor Roosevelt

I am grateful for the following things in my life: **A.M.**

_____
_____
_____

I will accomplish my "Big 3" today:

_____
_____
_____

This liberating belief will empower me today:

_____
_____
_____

Highlights of my day: **P.M.**

_____
_____
_____

Lessons learned:

_____
_____
_____

Did I accomplish my "Big 3" today? If not, why?

_____
_____

DAY 133   DATE: ___ / ___ / ___

"Respond to every call that excites your spirit."
—Rumi

I am grateful for the following things in my life: **A.M.**

_____

_____

_____

I will accomplish my "Big 3" today:

_____

_____

_____

This liberating belief will empower me today:

_____

_____

Highlights of my day: **P.M.**

_____

_____

_____

Lessons learned:

_____

_____

_____

Did I accomplish my "Big 3" today? If not, why?

_____

_____

DAY 134   DATE: ___ / ___ / ____

"A society grows great when old men plant trees whose shade they will never see." —Old Greek Proverb

I am grateful for the following things in my life: **A.M.**

_____
_____
_____

I will accomplish my "Big 3" today:

_____
_____
_____

This liberating belief will empower me today:

_____
_____

Highlights of my day: **P.M.**

_____
_____
_____

Lessons learned:

_____
_____
_____

Did I accomplish my "Big 3" today? If not, why?

_____
_____

DAY 135   DATE: ___ / ___ / ___

"A man is not old until his regrets take the place of his dreams."
—John Barrymore

I am grateful for the following things in my life: **A.M.**

_____
_____
_____

I will accomplish my "Big 3" today:

_____
_____
_____

This liberating belief will empower me today:

_____
_____

Highlights of my day: **P.M.**

_____
_____
_____

Lessons learned:

_____
_____
_____

Did I accomplish my "Big 3" today? If not, why?

_____
_____

DAY 136   DATE: ___ / ___ / ____

"A No. 2 pencil and a dream can take you anywhere."
—*Joyce Meyer*

I am grateful for the following things in my life: **A.M.**

_____
_____
_____

I will accomplish my "Big 3" today:

_____
_____
_____

This liberating belief will empower me today:

_____
_____
_____

Highlights of my day: **P.M.**

_____
_____
_____

Lessons learned:

_____
_____
_____

Did I accomplish my "Big 3" today? If not, why?

_____
_____

DAY 137   DATE: ___ / ___ / ___

"Become the victor, not the victim."
—*Dr. Stephany Coakley*

I am grateful for the following things in my life: **A.M.**

_____
_____
_____

I will accomplish my "Big 3" today:

_____
_____
_____

This liberating belief will empower me today:

_____
_____

Highlights of my day: **P.M.**

_____
_____
_____

Lessons learned:

_____
_____
_____

Did I accomplish my "Big 3" today? If not, why?

_____
_____

DAY 138   DATE: ___ / ___ / ____

"Don't let others rent space in your head."
—George Foreman

I am grateful for the following things in my life: **A.M.**

_____
_____

I will accomplish my "Big 3" today:

_____
_____

This liberating belief will empower me today:

_____
_____

Highlights of my day: **P.M.**

_____
_____

Lessons learned:

_____
_____

Did I accomplish my "Big 3" today? If not, why?

_____
_____

DAY 139   DATE: ___ / ___ / ____

"Do not withhold good from those to whom it is due, when it is in your power to act." — *Proverbs 3:27*

I am grateful for the following things in my life: **A.M.**

_____

_____

_____

I will accomplish my "Big 3" today:

_____

_____

_____

This liberating belief will empower me today:

_____

_____

Highlights of my day: **P.M.**

_____

_____

_____

Lessons learned:

_____

_____

_____

Did I accomplish my "Big 3" today? If not, why?

_____

_____

DAY 140 DATE: ___ / ___ / ____

"Lazy hands make for poverty, but diligent hands bring wealth." —Proverbs 10:4

I am grateful for the following things in my life: **A.M.**

_____
_____
_____

I will accomplish my "Big 3" today:

_____
_____
_____

This liberating belief will empower me today:

_____
_____
_____

Highlights of my day: **P.M.**

_____
_____
_____

Lessons learned:

_____
_____
_____

Did I accomplish my "Big 3" today? If not, why?

_____
_____

DAY 141   DATE: ___ / ___ / ___

"The happiest people in life are those who have an absolute devotion to mastery, achievement, and contribution."
—Dr. Gerald Bell

I am grateful for the following things in my life: **A.M.**

_____
_____
_____

I will accomplish my "Big 3" today:

_____
_____
_____

This liberating belief will empower me today:

_____
_____
_____

Highlights of my day: **P.M.**

_____
_____
_____

Lessons learned:

_____
_____
_____

Did I accomplish my "Big 3" today? If not, why?

_____
_____

DAY 142   DATE: ___ / ___ / _____

"Whoever disregards discipline comes to poverty and shame, but whoever heeds correction is honored." —Proverbs 13:18

I am grateful for the following things in my life: **A.M.**

___

I will accomplish my "Big 3" today:

___

This liberating belief will empower me today:

___

Highlights of my day: **P.M.**

___

Lessons learned:

___

Did I accomplish my "Big 3" today? If not, why?

DAY 143   DATE: ___ / ___ / ____

"This life is not a dress rehearsal. You only have one shot to get this thing right." —Kelly Doherty

I am grateful for the following things in my life: **A.M.**

_____
_____
_____

I will accomplish my "Big 3" today:

_____
_____
_____

This liberating belief will empower me today:

_____
_____

Highlights of my day: **P.M.**

_____
_____
_____

Lessons learned:

_____
_____
_____

Did I accomplish my "Big 3" today? If not, why?

_____
_____

DAY 144   DATE: ___ / ___ / ____

"If they can make penicillin out of moldy bread, they can sure make something out of you." —Muhammad Ali

I am grateful for the following things in my life: **A.M.**

_____
_____
_____

I will accomplish my "Big 3" today:

_____
_____
_____

This liberating belief will empower me today:

_____
_____
_____

Highlights of my day: **P.M.**

_____
_____
_____

Lessons learned:

_____
_____
_____

Did I accomplish my "Big 3" today? If not, why?

_____
_____

DAY 145 DATE: ___ / ___ / ___

"We suffer more in our imagination than in reality."
— Seneca

I am grateful for the following things in my life: **A.M.**

_____
_____

I will accomplish my "Big 3" today:

_____
_____

This liberating belief will empower me today:

_____
_____

Highlights of my day: **P.M.**

_____
_____

Lessons learned:

_____
_____

Did I accomplish my "Big 3" today? If not, why?

_____
_____

DAY 146　　　DATE: ___ / ___ / ___

"Discipline is the bridge between goals and accomplishments."
—Jennifer Holbrook

I am grateful for the following things in my life:　　**A.M.**

_____
_____
_____

I will accomplish my "Big 3" today:

_____
_____
_____

This liberating belief will empower me today:

_____
_____

Highlights of my day:　　**P.M.**

_____
_____
_____

Lessons learned:

_____
_____
_____

Did I accomplish my "Big 3" today? If not, why?

_____
_____

DAY 147 DATE: ___ / ___ / ___

"What it takes to win is simple, but it isn't easy."
—Marv Levy

I am grateful for the following things in my life: **A.M.**

_____
_____
_____

I will accomplish my "Big 3" today:

_____
_____
_____

This liberating belief will empower me today:

_____
_____

Highlights of my day: **P.M.**

_____
_____
_____

Lessons learned:

_____
_____
_____

Did I accomplish my "Big 3" today? If not, why?

_____
_____

DAY 148   DATE: ___ / ___ / ____

"Give without remembering, take without forgetting."
—*Brian Tracy*

I am grateful for the following things in my life: **A.M.**

_____
_____
_____

I will accomplish my "Big 3" today:

_____
_____
_____

This liberating belief will empower me today:

_____
_____
_____

Highlights of my day: **P.M.**

_____
_____
_____

Lessons learned:

_____
_____
_____

Did I accomplish my "Big 3" today? If not, why?

_____
_____

DAY 149   DATE: ___ / ___ / ____

"Don't let your history get in the way of your destiny."
— *Pastor Veach*

I am grateful for the following things in my life: **A.M.**

_____
_____
_____

I will accomplish my "Big 3" today:

_____
_____
_____

This liberating belief will empower me today:

_____
_____

Highlights of my day: **P.M.**

_____
_____
_____

Lessons learned:

_____
_____
_____

Did I accomplish my "Big 3" today? If not, why?

_____
_____

DAY 150   DATE: ___ / ___ / ____

"The secret to your future is hidden in your daily routine."
—John Lucas

I am grateful for the following things in my life: **A.M.**

_____
_____
_____

I will accomplish my "Big 3" today:

_____
_____
_____

This liberating belief will empower me today:

_____
_____
_____

Highlights of my day: **P.M.**

_____
_____
_____

Lessons learned:

_____
_____
_____

Did I accomplish my "Big 3" today? If not, why?

_____
_____

Keep the Momentum Going!

Congratulations! You've reached the 150 day mark in your the *Time Out Journal*—an incredible testament to your commitment to personal growth, reflection, and leadership development.

Consistency is the key to lasting transformation, and you've been showing up for yourself every day. Don't let this momentum slip! Now is the perfect time to order your next the *Time Out Journal* so you can continue this powerful journey without interruption.

Growth doesn't happen overnight—it's the result of daily reflection, intentionality, and learning from experience. Keep building on the progress you've made, and set yourself up for success by securing your next journal today.

Take action now! Visit www.dohertycoaching.com to order your next the *Time Out Journal* and continue to *Learn & Grow*.

Gratitude Shifts Everything

 A message from Coach Doherty

After leaving UNC, I was bitter. I focused on what I'd lost—my job, my reputation, my sense of purpose. It brought me to my knees. What do you do when you are on your knees? Pray. My failure brought me closer to God. I learned to lean on His understanding. God doesn't promise us a smooth path, but hardship to bring us closer to Him. I learned to thank Him for the setbacks because it forced me to grow as a person, as a leader and as a Christian.

I started noticing small things—a supportive family, a new opportunity, even just a good cup of coffee. Gratitude didn't change my circumstances, but it changed how I saw them.

When you focus on what's missing, you feel empty. But when you focus on your blessings, you feel abundant. Gratitude is a mindset that shifts your entire outlook on life.

Reflection:

- ➢ What are three things you're grateful for right now?
- ➢ How can you make gratitude a daily practice?
- ➢ When you face challenges, how can you find something to be thankful for?

Gratitude doesn't just reflect your life—it transforms it.

DAY 151 DATE: ___ / ___ / ___

"The tongue has no bones, but is strong enough to break a heart! So be careful with your words." —Buddha

I am grateful for the following things in my life: **A.M.**

_____

_____

_____

I will accomplish my "Big 3" today:

_____

_____

_____

This liberating belief will empower me today:

_____

_____

Highlights of my day: **P.M.**

_____

_____

_____

Lessons learned:

_____

_____

_____

Did I accomplish my "Big 3" today? If not, why?

_____

_____

DAY 152   DATE: ___ / ___ / _____

"Consider it pure joy, my brothers, whenever you face trials of many kinds, because you know that the testing of your faith develops perseverance." —James 1:2-3

I am grateful for the following things in my life: **A.M.**

_____
_____
_____

I will accomplish my "Big 3" today:

_____
_____
_____

This liberating belief will empower me today:

_____
_____

Highlights of my day: **P.M.**

_____
_____
_____

Lessons learned:

_____
_____
_____

Did I accomplish my "Big 3" today? If not, why?

_____
_____

DAY 153   DATE: ___ / ___ / ___

> *"Momentum is messy."*
> —Jon Acuff

I am grateful for the following things in my life: **A.M.**

_____
_____
_____

I will accomplish my "Big 3" today:

_____
_____
_____

This liberating belief will empower me today:

_____
_____
_____

Highlights of my day: **P.M.**

_____
_____
_____

Lessons learned:

_____
_____
_____

Did I accomplish my "Big 3" today? If not, why?

_____
_____

DAY 154   DATE: ___ / ___ / ____

"The presence of anxiety is unavoidable, but the prison of anxiety is optional." —Max Lucado

I am grateful for the following things in my life: **A.M.**

_____
_____
_____

I will accomplish my "Big 3" today:

_____
_____
_____

This liberating belief will empower me today:

_____
_____
_____

Highlights of my day: **P.M.**

_____
_____
_____

Lessons learned:

_____
_____
_____

Did I accomplish my "Big 3" today? If not, why?

_____
_____

DAY 155   DATE: ___ / ___ / _____

"Surround yourself with people strong enough to change your mind." —John Wooden

I am grateful for the following things in my life: **A.M.**

_____
_____
_____

I will accomplish my "Big 3" today:

_____
_____
_____

This liberating belief will empower me today:

_____
_____

Highlights of my day: **P.M.**

_____
_____
_____

Lessons learned:

_____
_____
_____

Did I accomplish my "Big 3" today? If not, why?

_____
_____

DAY 156 DATE: ___ / ___ / ___

"He who is not courageous enough to take risks will accomplish nothing in life." —Muhammad Ali

I am grateful for the following things in my life: **A.M.**

_____
_____
_____

I will accomplish my "Big 3" today:

_____
_____
_____

This liberating belief will empower me today:

_____
_____
_____

Highlights of my day: **P.M.**

_____
_____
_____

Lessons learned:

_____
_____
_____

Did I accomplish my "Big 3" today? If not, why?

_____
_____

DAY 157 DATE: ___ / ___ / ___

"Don't let your failures go to waste."
—*Unknown*

I am grateful for the following things in my life: **A.M.**

_____
_____

I will accomplish my "Big 3" today:

_____
_____

This liberating belief will empower me today:

_____
_____

Highlights of my day: **P.M.**

_____
_____

Lessons learned:

_____
_____

Did I accomplish my "Big 3" today? If not, why?

_____
_____

DAY 158   DATE: ___ / ___ / ____

"And whether or not it is clear to you, no doubt the universe is unfolding as it should. Therefore, be at peace with God, whatever you conceive Him to be." —Max Ehrmann

I am grateful for the following things in my life: **A.M.**

_____

_____

_____

I will accomplish my "Big 3" today:

_____

_____

_____

This liberating belief will empower me today:

_____

_____

Highlights of my day: **P.M.**

_____

_____

_____

Lessons learned:

_____

_____

_____

Did I accomplish my "Big 3" today? If not, why?

_____

_____

DAY 159   DATE: ___ / ___ / ____

"I demolish my bridges behind me... then there is no choice but to move." —Fridtjof Nansen

I am grateful for the following things in my life: **A.M.**

_____
_____
_____

I will accomplish my "Big 3" today:

_____
_____
_____

This liberating belief will empower me today:

_____
_____

Highlights of my day: **P.M.**

_____
_____
_____

Lessons learned:

_____
_____

Did I accomplish my "Big 3" today? If not, why?

_____
_____

DAY 160　　　DATE: ___ / ___ / ____

"Define your unique talent or gift, develop it to the fullest, and give it away every day." —Don Meyer

I am grateful for the following things in my life:　　**A.M.**

_____
_____
_____

I will accomplish my "Big 3" today:

_____
_____
_____

This liberating belief will empower me today:

_____
_____
_____

Highlights of my day:　　**P.M.**

_____
_____
_____

Lessons learned:

_____
_____
_____

Did I accomplish my "Big 3" today? If not, why?

_____
_____

DAY 161   DATE: ___ / ___ / _____

"I will not let anyone walk through my mind with their dirty feet." —Gandhi

I am grateful for the following things in my life: **A.M.**

_____
_____
_____

I will accomplish my "Big 3" today:

_____
_____
_____

This liberating belief will empower me today:

_____
_____
_____

Highlights of my day: **P.M.**

_____
_____
_____

Lessons learned:

_____
_____
_____

Did I accomplish my "Big 3" today? If not, why?

_____
_____

DAY 162 DATE: ___ / ___ / _____

"Silence is one of the great arts of conversation."
—*Cicero*

I am grateful for the following things in my life: **A.M.**

_____
_____
_____

I will accomplish my "Big 3" today:

_____
_____
_____

This liberating belief will empower me today:

_____
_____
_____

Highlights of my day: **P.M.**

_____
_____
_____

Lessons learned:

_____
_____
_____

Did I accomplish my "Big 3" today? If not, why?

_____
_____

DAY 163   DATE: ___ / ___ / _____

"Make no little plans. They have no magic to stir men's blood. Make big plans; aim high in hope and work." —Daniel Burnham

I am grateful for the following things in my life: **A.M.**

_____
_____
_____

I will accomplish my "Big 3" today:

_____
_____
_____

This liberating belief will empower me today:

_____
_____

Highlights of my day: **P.M.**

_____
_____
_____

Lessons learned:

_____
_____
_____

Did I accomplish my "Big 3" today? If not, why?

_____
_____

DAY 164   DATE: ___ / ___ / ___

"Live everyday like it's your last because someday you're going to be right." —Muhammad Ali

I am grateful for the following things in my life: **A.M.**

_____
_____
_____

I will accomplish my "Big 3" today:

_____
_____
_____

This liberating belief will empower me today:

_____
_____
_____

Highlights of my day: **P.M.**

_____
_____
_____

Lessons learned:

_____
_____
_____

Did I accomplish my "Big 3" today? If not, why?

_____
_____

DAY 165　　DATE: ___ / ___ / _____

"In his heart a man plans his course, but the Lord determines his steps." —Proverbs 16:9

I am grateful for the following things in my life:　**A.M.**

_____
_____
_____

I will accomplish my "Big 3" today:

_____
_____
_____

This liberating belief will empower me today:

_____
_____

Highlights of my day:　**P.M.**

_____
_____
_____

Lessons learned:

_____
_____
_____

Did I accomplish my "Big 3" today? If not, why?

_____
_____

DAY 166　　　DATE: ___ / ___ / _____

"Best to build relationships before you need them."
—Keith Ferrazzi

I am grateful for the following things in my life:　**A.M.**

_____
_____
_____

I will accomplish my "Big 3" today:

_____
_____
_____

This liberating belief will empower me today:

_____
_____
_____

Highlights of my day:　**P.M.**

_____
_____
_____

Lessons learned:

_____
_____
_____

Did I accomplish my "Big 3" today? If not, why?

_____
_____

DAY 167   DATE: ___ / ___ / ____

"When we push back from feedback we move away from a better version of ourselves." —Pastor Adam Johnson

I am grateful for the following things in my life: **A.M.**

_____
_____
_____

I will accomplish my "Big 3" today:

_____
_____
_____

This liberating belief will empower me today:

_____
_____

Highlights of my day: **P.M.**

_____
_____
_____

Lessons learned:

_____
_____
_____

Did I accomplish my "Big 3" today? If not, why?

_____
_____

DAY 168　　　DATE: ___ / ___ / _____

"Buy the truth and do not sell it—wisdom, instruction and insight as well." —Proverbs 23:23

I am grateful for the following things in my life:　**A.M.**

_____

_____

_____

I will accomplish my "Big 3" today:

_____

_____

_____

This liberating belief will empower me today:

_____

_____

_____

Highlights of my day:　**P.M.**

_____

_____

_____

Lessons learned:

_____

_____

_____

Did I accomplish my "Big 3" today? If not, why?

_____

_____

DAY 169   DATE: ___ / ___ / _____

"You are the average of the five people you spend the most time with." —Jim Rohn

I am grateful for the following things in my life: **A.M.**

_____
_____
_____

I will accomplish my "Big 3" today:

_____
_____
_____

This liberating belief will empower me today:

_____
_____
_____

Highlights of my day: **P.M.**

_____
_____
_____

Lessons learned:

_____
_____
_____

Did I accomplish my "Big 3" today? If not, why?

_____
_____

DAY 170 DATE: ___ / ___ / _____

"I have always tried to keep my confidence and optimism up, no matter how difficult the situation." —Colin Powell

I am grateful for the following things in my life: **A.M.**

_____
_____
_____

I will accomplish my "Big 3" today:

_____
_____
_____

This liberating belief will empower me today:

_____
_____
_____

Highlights of my day: **P.M.**

_____
_____
_____

Lessons learned:

_____
_____
_____

Did I accomplish my "Big 3" today? If not, why?

_____
_____

DAY 171   DATE: ___ / ___ / ___

"What has happened to you has also happened for you."
— Oprah Winfrey

I am grateful for the following things in my life: **A.M.**

_____
_____
_____

I will accomplish my "Big 3" today:

_____
_____
_____

This liberating belief will empower me today:

_____
_____
_____

Highlights of my day: **P.M.**

_____
_____
_____

Lessons learned:

_____
_____
_____

Did I accomplish my "Big 3" today? If not, why?

_____
_____

DAY 172   DATE: ___ / ___ / ___

"Unless we change our direction, we are likely to end up where we are headed." —Dan Wertenberg

I am grateful for the following things in my life: **A.M.**

_____
_____
_____

I will accomplish my "Big 3" today:

_____
_____
_____

This liberating belief will empower me today:

_____
_____
_____

Highlights of my day: **P.M.**

_____
_____
_____

Lessons learned:

_____
_____
_____

Did I accomplish my "Big 3" today? If not, why?

_____
_____

DAY 173   DATE: ___ / ___ / _____

"The person that challenges you and holds you accountable loves you more than the person that watches you stay the same and settle for mediocrity." —Elizabeth Gush

I am grateful for the following things in my life: **A.M.**

_____

_____

I will accomplish my "Big 3" today:

_____

_____

This liberating belief will empower me today:

_____

_____

Highlights of my day: **P.M.**

_____

_____

Lessons learned:

_____

_____

Did I accomplish my "Big 3" today? If not, why?

_____

_____

DAY 174   DATE: ___ / ___ / ___

"Between stimulus and response, there is a space. In that space is our power to choose our response. In our response lies our growth and our freedom." —Viktor Frankl

I am grateful for the following things in my life: **A.M.**

_____
_____
_____

I will accomplish my "Big 3" today:

_____
_____
_____

This liberating belief will empower me today:

_____
_____

Highlights of my day: **P.M.**

_____
_____
_____

Lessons learned:

_____
_____
_____

Did I accomplish my "Big 3" today? If not, why?

_____
_____

DAY 175 DATE: ___ / ___ / _____

"Optimism is true moral courage."
— *Shackleton's Way*

I am grateful for the following things in my life: **A.M.**

_____
_____
_____

I will accomplish my "Big 3" today:

_____
_____
_____

This liberating belief will empower me today:

_____
_____

Highlights of my day: **P.M.**

_____
_____
_____

Lessons learned:

_____
_____
_____

Did I accomplish my "Big 3" today? If not, why?

_____
_____

DAY 176   DATE: ___ / ___ / ___

"It's not what you say, it's how you say it."
—*Mary Doherty*

I am grateful for the following things in my life: **A.M.**

_____
_____
_____

I will accomplish my "Big 3" today:

_____
_____
_____

This liberating belief will empower me today:

_____
_____

Highlights of my day: **P.M.**

_____
_____
_____

Lessons learned:

_____
_____
_____

Did I accomplish my "Big 3" today? If not, why?

_____
_____

DAY 177   DATE: ___ / ___ / ____

"There are three extremely hard things: steel, a diamond, and to know oneself." —Ben Franklin

I am grateful for the following things in my life: **A.M.**

_____
_____
_____

I will accomplish my "Big 3" today:

_____
_____
_____

This liberating belief will empower me today:

_____
_____

Highlights of my day: **P.M.**

_____
_____
_____

Lessons learned:

_____
_____
_____

Did I accomplish my "Big 3" today? If not, why?

_____
_____

DAY 178   DATE: ___ / ___ / ___

"Bloom where you are planted."
—Saint Francis de Sales

I am grateful for the following things in my life: **A.M.**

_____
_____
_____

I will accomplish my "Big 3" today:

_____
_____
_____

This liberating belief will empower me today:

_____
_____
_____

Highlights of my day: **P.M.**

_____
_____
_____

Lessons learned:

_____
_____
_____

Did I accomplish my "Big 3" today? If not, why?

_____
_____

DAY 179   DATE: ___ / ___ / ___

"I've learned that people will forget what you said, people will forget what you did, but people will never forget how you made them feel." —Maya Angelou

I am grateful for the following things in my life: **A.M.**

_____
_____
_____

I will accomplish my "Big 3" today:

_____
_____
_____

This liberating belief will empower me today:

_____
_____

Highlights of my day: **P.M.**

_____
_____
_____

Lessons learned:

_____
_____
_____

Did I accomplish my "Big 3" today? If not, why?

_____
_____

DAY 180   DATE: ___ / ___ / _____

"In every contest, there comes a moment that separates winning from losing. The true warriors understand and seize that moment." —Pat Riley

I am grateful for the following things in my life: **A.M.**

_____
_____
_____

I will accomplish my "Big 3" today:

_____
_____
_____

This liberating belief will empower me today:

_____
_____

Highlights of my day: **P.M.**

_____
_____
_____

Lessons learned:

_____
_____
_____

Did I accomplish my "Big 3" today? If not, why?

_____
_____

Congratulations!

You've completed 180 days of journaling—a testament to your commitment to growth, self-awareness, and intentional leadership. Every page you've filled has been a step forward, shaping the mindset and habits that separate great leaders from the rest.

Reflection: The Best Keep Getting Better

A message from Coach Doherty

The greatest athletes, CEOs, and leaders all have one thing in common - they never stop learning. You've put in the time journaling, reflecting, and setting goals.

Now, ask yourself:

Could I grow faster with the right coaching?

If the answer is "yes," let's start that conversation.

Visit www.dohertycoaching.com and take your leadership to the next level.

BOOKS BY **MATT DOHERTY**

AND HIS FORTHCOMING BOOK…

The Time Out Leader
Releasing in 2026

Visit **www.dohertycoaching.com** for books and resources.

ABOUT THE AUTHOR

Coach Matt Doherty is a nationally recognized motivational speaker, best-selling author, media personality, and executive coach. He appeared on *New to the Street* on Bloomberg TV in 2023-2024 and on *The Rebound with Matt Doherty* on The First TV. Currently, Coach Matt appears regularly on WBT Charlotte and his own YouTube channel featuring The Rebound.

In addition to his keynotes and trainings, he guides corporations, C-suite managers, sales executives, and sports coaches to develop their leadership skills, culture, and team dynamics.

As a starter of the 1982 National Championship team with Michael Jordan at UNC, he began his leadership journey under the legendary Dean Smith. He went on to be the Head Coach at Notre Dame and North Carolina, and in 2001 led the team to the ACC Regular Season Championship and was named the AP National Coach of the Year.

Coach Doherty also was the Head Coach at FAU and SMU, in addition to working with ESPN, the Indiana Pacers, and the Atlantic 10 Conference. His mission is to *"Learn & Grow"* every day and his leadership journey took him to the UVA Darden School of Business and The Wharton School. He is committed to sharing universal teachings and lessons from the basketball court to the boardroom, all with actionable ideas that will work for you. Matt will provide the game plan... the rest is up to you.

Representing a community of authors whose books have collectively sold hundreds of millions of copies, the founders of The Gray + Miller Agency launched Maison Vero, a professional publishing house that partners with rising authors to bring their thought leadership to the world. Our representation covers every aspect of thought leadership, including U.S. senators, governors, and ambassadors, billionaire founders and entrepreneurs, researchers, academics, scientists, consultants, practitioners, social influencers, C-suite leaders, adventurers, professional athletes, artists, and creators. We partner with thought leaders and world changers like you who have a story to tell. By bringing decades of professional expertise to our clients, we are charting a new path in a timeless industry that transcends publishing norms, transforming powerful thoughts into impactful books that inspire minds, ignite hearts, and open doors.

Visit **maisonvero.com** to view our growing list of authors, or to submit a proposal for publication consideration.

Follow Maison Vero for insight and inspiration on social media:

 MaisonVero    MaisonVero    MaisonVeroPublishing

For information about special discounts for bulk purchases, please call 1-949-333-4872 or email info@graymilleragency.com.

Maison Vero is a partner brand of The Gray + Miller Agency, a speaking, literary, and talent consortium. For more information on the talent represented by The Gray + Miller Agency, or to bring any of our thought leaders to your organization or live event, please visit our website at **graymilleragency.com**.

www.ingramcontent.com/pod-product-compliance
Lightning Source LLC
Chambersburg PA
CBHW050732010526
44107CB00010B/825